Ladies Who Drink

A STYLISHLY SPIRITED GUIDE
TO MIXED DRINKS AND SMALL BITES

ANNE KEENAN HIGGINS

Text by Marisa Bulzone

RUNNING PRESS
PHILADELPHIA

Running Press
Hachette Book Group
1290 Avenue of the Americas, New York, NY 10104
www.runningpress.com
@Running_Press

Printed in China

Published by Running Press, an imprint of Perseus Books, LLC,
a subsidiary of Hachette Book Group, Inc.

The Hachette Speakers Bureau provides a wide range
of authors for speaking events. To find out more, go to
www.hachettespeakersbureau.com or call (866) 376-6591.

The publisher is not responsible for websites
(or their content) that are not owned by the publisher.

Print book cover and interior design
by Amanda Richmond with Anne Keenan Higgins

Library of Congress Control Number: 2017940263

ISBNs: 978-0-7624-6188-2 (hardcover), 978-0-7624-6189-9 (ebook)

LEO

10 9 8 7 6 5 4 3 2 1

TO MY FAVORITE
MIXOLOGIST,
JASON.

Contents

Introduction

SO WHAT SHALL WE HAVE TO DRINK? IN TIMES PAST
when you got together with friends, there probably were a few bottles of
wine and maybe some cheese and crackers (we won't mention the keg of
beer in the backyard). Today, you might be meeting in chic bars for cocktails and taking your snack menu up a notch or two.

Whether you call it a craft cocktail, artisanal mixology, or simply a good
drink, any quality bar and most restaurants now feature a specialty cocktail
menu that rivals the best wine list. In the hands of a skilled bartender,
these signature drinks may feature an equally long list of ingredients and
increasingly elaborate garnishes. It's all upped the ante on serving cocktails
at home—but there's no need to be intimidated.

When guests arrive, go ahead and ask them, "Would you like a drink?"
This collection of tasty cocktail recipes and simple food pairings will prepare you for their answer. The cocktails, both time-honored and original,
are not overly complicated and do not call for exotic ingredients; likewise,
the advice and instructions offered are meant to take you by the hand and
demystify the process. Really, mixing cocktails doesn't have to be such
serious business—let's focus on our friends and having fun. The empha-
sis in this collection is on fresh flavors and natural ingredients. The food
suggestions require little in the way of cooking skills, and many make
creative use of store-bought items.

Whether you're hosting the book club or having friends in for a holiday toast, setting up the Netflix queue or getting in the mood for your
next vacation, you'll find cocktail and pairing ideas to suit a number of
themes. The details on five classic cocktails and their variations will have

you prepared for any occasion and you can even invent your own signature drink by following the advice on page 182.

Consider these recipes as perfect excuses to gather friends and family, raise a glass, and share a toast and a few laughs. That's the true definition of hours spent happily.

Cheers! Skål! L'Chaim! Sláinte! Salute!

Let's Get the Party Started

WHAT'S ON YOUR COCKTAIL CART? A HOME BAR BUILT
for casual entertaining doesn't need to be an elaborate affair. Find an out-
of-the-way spot in your living space—a dedicated bookshelf or cabinet
nook—to safely store a few bottles, a shaker, a shot glass, perhaps a small
ice bucket and some specialty glassware, and you're set.

If you love the idea of a cocktail cart, you'll find lots to choose from
on home décor sites, but also check out yard sales and flea markets for
great-looking vintage carts from the 1950s and '60s.

When it comes to the bottles, start with what you, your friends, and your
family like to drink and plan from there. If your liquor of choice is bourbon,
that's your first bottle. Your best friend—the one who's over at least one or
two nights a week? If she likes gin, that's your next bottle. Be a good friend
and buy her favorite brand while you're at it. If your family lives nearby and
your dad likes tequila, he'll appreciate seeing a bottle when he drops in.

You can cover most impromptu cocktail situations with three bottles:
vodka, gin, and bourbon. If you daydream about your next island vacation,
add a bottle of rum. If your taste runs more to Cabo or Cancun, swap out
the rum for tequila. Add a nice bottle of red wine, and a bottle of white, a
bottle of Angostura bitters (see page 24), and always have a few bottles of
sparkling water, some lemons and limes in the fridge, and ice cubes in the
freezer. If you're prone to toasts, keep a bottle of Champagne or sparkling
wine (see page 181) in the fridge, too.

8

To expand your mixology universe, add some liqueurs or amari. *Liqueurs* are low-alcohol distilled spirits, flavored with fruit, herbs, or floral extracts, and are typically sweet. There are hundreds of liqueurs available from around the world, in flavors from apple and orange to elderflower and ginger.

Liqueurs tend to be pricey, but some of the most popular ones are available in small bottles that are more affordable and much more practical. Vermouth—wine fortified with a variety of botanicals—is an essential ingredient in many classic cocktails, including the Martini (page 66) and the Manhattan (page 52). It's available in white and red, sweet and dry versions; choose a white, sweet vermouth for your basic bar.

Many liqueurs have long and storied histories, and they tend to rise and fall in popularity according to mixology trends. Follow your own taste and stock only those that you find in your favorite cocktails. Some of the most popular and widely used are Cointreau (with bitter orange flavor), St-Germain Elderflower (a citrusy floral, made from elderflower), and chartreuse in both yellow and green versions (intensely herbal).

Amari are a group of aperitif liqueurs characterized by their bitter flavors. These herbal blends have centuries-old medicinal roots in Italy, France, and Germany and are popular components in artisanal cocktails. The brilliant red Campari, infused with bitter herbs, is a good addition to the home bar; serve it with sparkling water, or as part of the classic Negroni (page 125). Aperol, with notes of bitter orange and rhubarb, and Cynar, with its distinctive artichoke flavor, are other popular amari.

Don't break your budget to set up your home bar, but do buy the best you can afford. While it's true that very top shelf brands are designed for sipping solo, it's a myth to think that a mixed drink doesn't benefit from at least the middle shelf. The better the quality of the liquor, the better the quality of your cocktails, so shop around and keep an eye out for specials. Most good liquor stores—even the big box kind—have knowledgeable staff who can guide you to the smartest purchase. Liquor doesn't spoil, and with craft cocktails at bars costing an average of $10 to $20 each, you'll actually be making a good investment.

Brake for Estate Sales

Estate and even yard sales can be a home entertainer's best friend. Not only might you score a cool retro bar cart, these house-clearing bazaars are a great source for vintage cocktail sets and other glassware, serving bowls and trays, and sometimes full, never-opened bottles of liquor—all at rock-bottom prices.

THE NOT-SO-SERIOUS
BUSINESS OF GLASSWARE

SERIOUS MIXOLOGY GUIDES CAN LIST MORE THAN
twenty different glasses designed to hold specific types of cocktails. That's
an ambitious inventory even if your last name is Crawley and you live at
Downton Abbey. Once again, start small and keep things simple.

The tall and narrow highball glass (also known as a Collins glass,
although some differentiate between the two) holds 8 to 10 ounces and
is most commonly called for in recipes for drinks served over lots of ice
and topped with tonic or sparkling water, like a Gin and Tonic (page 82).
If your everyday tall drinking glasses aren't made of plastic and mono-
grammed with Disney characters, they'll usually suffice.

The rocks glass (or old-fashioned glass) holds 5 to 10 ounces; the double
old-fashioned glass can hold up to 13 ounces. Chances are that same set
of everyday drinking glasses of yours also contains glasses of this size. In a
pinch—despite it being cocktail heresy—a stemless wine glass would also
serve well here. Just be sure that your ice cubes fit through the rim.

The cocktail glass (also known as a martini glass) is designed to hold
martinis and other cocktails served without ice. Contemporary models
will hold 5½ ounces; vintage glassware is often smaller. (See Reinventing
the Nick & Nora Glass, page 13.) If martinis are your thing, then you
should have a set of these glasses. The coupe glass, which also holds 5½
ounces, can be used for martini-style cocktails as well as Champagne,
making them a more practical style of specialty glassware. Even more
practical? Look for sets in secondhand shops, where you may find actual
crystal for a low price.

The Champagne flute is a tall, narrow wine glass that holds 8 ounces of
bubbly. Traditionally used for toasting, they are, however, a single-use item.

coupe

martini

nick & nora

rocks

moscow mule

snifter

margarita

flute

pilsner

port

highball

If you always have a bottle of Champagne in the fridge, you might want to add these to your gift registry. Otherwise, consider the more user-friendly coupe described previously.

Margarita glasses, brandy snifters, port glasses, pilsners (for beer), and copper mugs (for Moscow Mules, see page 160) are all dedicated to a specific style of drink. If you serve any of these with frequency, by all means add them to your collection.

Reinventing the Nick & Nora Glass

Nick and Nora Charles, the super-stylish husband-and-wife detective team made famous by William Powell and Myrna Loy in six *Thin Man* movies of the 1930s and '40s, loved cocktails almost as much as they did each other. Watch the films and, in addition to lusting after Myrna's fabulous wardrobe, you'll see them sipping from a decidedly different shape of cocktail glass. Deeper than a coupe, rounder than a martini, these early cocktail glasses were closer to a small, stemmed wine glass (holding about two ounces of liquid). The renaissance of these elegant glasses is attributed to mixologist Audrey Saunders, who reintroduced them at the launch of her groundbreaking New York cocktail lounge Pegu Club in 2005. New versions (many imprinted with vintage patterns) can now be found wherever cocktail glassware is sold, but in a very modern six-ounce capacity.

THE BASIC BAR TOOLS

YOU CAN CHOOSE FROM A WIDE RANGE OF BAR TOOLS in an equally wide range of price points, but there are just a few necessary items needed for making a good cocktail, and some can already be found in your kitchen, no doubt!

There are various types of cocktail shakers available; no matter what style you choose, a shaker is a necessary item for the bar cart. The Cobbler cocktail shaker is usually all stainless-steel, with a built-in strainer and a metal cap. The Boston shaker has a stainless-steel bottom and a glass top. If you choose a Boston shaker, you will need a separate strainer, but you can use the glass portion as a mixing pitcher for cocktails that are not shaken, but stirred. (For tips on how to use a shaker, see page 17.)

A shaken cocktail must be strained of its ice and any other solids that might have been added to the barrel (mint or other herbs, fruit pulp, and the like). If the strainer isn't built in, there are two choices: the Hawthorne strainer, which has a metal coil around the edge that grips tightly to the shaker, and the Julep strainer, which resembles a flat, wide slotted spoon with a short handle.

Accurate measuring makes quality cocktails, and for that you'll need a shot glass or jigger. Both are expected to hold 1½ ounces of liquid, but they can vary. And although shot glasses are handy for drinking shots, OXO produces a mini angled measuring jigger in stainless steel that makes it very easy to see incremental measures up to 2 ounces.

A small glass pitcher in which to stir drinks that aren't shaken can be helpful. A long-handled bar spoon is designed to stir cocktails, but you could use a long drinking straw (or even a single chopstick) in a pinch.

A muddler is a small wooden baton used to crush fruit or herbs in the bottom of a glass. A narrow wooden spoon works just fine here.

Take a sharp paring knife, a peeler, a citrus reamer or handheld juicer, and a small cutting board from the kitchen; while you're there, grab a bowl to hold some ice (see page 15).

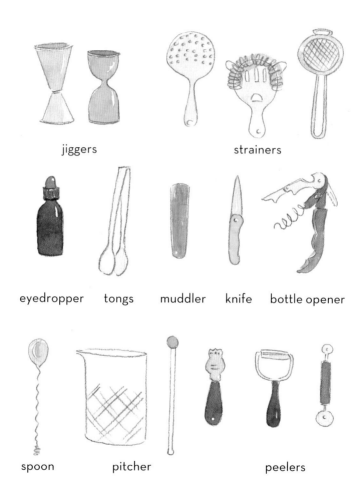

jiggers   strainers

eyedropper   tongs   muddler   knife   bottle opener

spoon   pitcher   peelers

Boston shaker   Cobbler shakers

Shaken, Not Stirred

Each recipe will guide you as to whether or not a drink should be shaken, but here are a few general tips:

- Unless directed otherwise, fill the shaker base about three-quarters full with ice, then add your ingredients.

- The melted ice should add about 1 ounce of liquid to your cocktail.

- The purpose of shaking a cocktail is to mix the ingredients and to make the liquid cold. That means the shaker will get cold, too, so wrap the shaker in a kitchen towel to keep your hands from freezing.

- Hold tightly to the top and shake, shake, shake away (it's great for toning your upper arms) for 8 to 12 seconds, unless otherwise specified. For drinks made with egg whites, shake the ingredients for 5 to 7 seconds before adding the ice, then shake for about 12 seconds more.

- If, after shaking, the metal lid on a Cobbler shaker gets stuck, don't panic. Once you've made the cocktail, the metal is cold and contracted. It has also created suction, so you need to rock it back and forth instead of twisting or pulling it off. If that doesn't work, try wrapping a large rubber band (or a jar opener) around the top to give you a better grip, or dampen a paper towel with hot water and wrap it around the top to expand the metal. If the two pieces of your Boston shaker get stuck together, give it a smack at the top of the tin.

- For a shaken cocktail served over ice, always strain the cocktail over fresh ice in the glass, discarding the ice left behind in the shaker.

Stirred, Not Shaken

As with shaking, the purpose of stirring a cocktail is to mix the ingredients and get them cold without too much dilution.

• Fill the mixing glass or pitcher about two-thirds full with a mixture of cracked and cubed ice.

• Stir gently but completely with a long-handled spoon for about 12 seconds.

• For a stirred cocktail served over ice, always strain the cocktail over fresh ice in the glass, discarding the ice left behind in the mixing glass.

THE TWO Cs OF ICE: CUT AND CLARITY

ONE OF THE HALLMARKS OF A HIGH-QUALITY CRAFT cocktail program is the clarity of its ice. Bar owners spend a pretty penny sourcing ice that's crystal clear, or buying special equipment to make their own. That large block or sphere looks great in your glass, but there's a practical reason behind it that you should appreciate: both the size and the clarity make the ice melt more slowly, thereby diluting your drink less.

You'll find many an online treatise explaining how to achieve frozen clarity, but here's a simple way to up your ice game at home. Start with distilled water, then boil it—twice—letting it cool after each boiling. Once the water has cooled the second time, fill your ice cube trays half full. If you like, once the cubes are frozen, add the remaining water to fill the trays the rest of the way.

Silicone ice trays are available in all sizes and shapes, so choose what works best for you, your freezer—and your glassware. If you're thinking of making very large cubes or spheres, first make sure they will fit in your serving glasses!

BE PREPARED TO PARTY

WHILE MOST OF WHAT'S DESCRIBED IN THIS BOOK IS best for time spent with a few good friends, there will be some times when you find yourself with a crowd. Here's a handy guide:

• Choose three or four signature drinks for the party. Mix the main ingredients in pitchers—minus anything bubbly—and store them in the fridge until party time. See page 144 for more advice on making pitcher cocktails.

• Plan on three drinks per person. (You know your guests: some will drink more; some will drink less.)

• Have two pounds of ice available per guest. (This is a good time to borrow a cooler if you don't have one.)

• If you plan on making individual cocktails, keep in mind that a 750-ml bottle of alcohol makes about 15 cocktails.

• Always—*always*—have a few fun, non-alcoholic options available.

STAY FRESH

COCKTAILS DO NOT SUCCEED BY ALCOHOL ALONE.
Mixers include all manner of sparkling ingredients, from water to soda to wine, fruit and vegetable juices, sugar and flavored syrups, and bitters.

Fruit and vegetable juices are always freshly squeezed. No exceptions.

When a cocktail calls for carbonation, you have a few bubbly choices: seltzer water, club soda, and mineral water all bring effervescence to the glass with no added flavor. The recipes in this book call for "sparkling water," but it's your choice which to use. Seltzer water is the cheapest (and if you have a SodaStream or something similar, it's always available, too); club soda contains a few artificial ingredients that up its sodium level; mineral water (think Perrier) is naturally carbonated with a slightly more gentle bubble. It's the most expensive and best reserved for drinking on its own.

Each of these sparkling waters is available in flavored versions. Should you want to use them to emphasize the lime, orange, or grapefruit flavors in a drink, feel free to give it a try, but this is not a substitute for the natural juice specified in the recipe.

Tonic water is actually a soda, and despite its bitter flavor (which comes from the main ingredient of quinine), most commercial brands contain a lot of high fructose corn syrup. If you're a fan of tonic-based drinks (like the Gin and Tonic, page 82), it's worth it to sample some of the premium brands like Fever-Tree, Q, and Jack Rudy, which have developed their recipes to include quality blends of botanicals and natural sugars. Fever-Tree also has a "naturally light" tonic, with about half the calories of their original. Those with a DIY bent may want to try making tonic at home.

It's not difficult to do, but cocktail expert Camper English warns of studies that indicate ingesting too much cinchona bark (from which quinine is derived) can lead to cinchonism, which causes fever, dizziness, and nausea among other symptoms. The concern is that many home recipes use a powdered form of the bark, which is too fine to be thoroughly strained from the final product.

At their most basic, cocktails are based on a ratio of alcohol to sour to sweet. The sweet usually comes in the form of simple syrup, a mixture of sugar and water. You can buy simple syrup in a wide variety of interesting flavors, but stick to small-batch artisanal brands and always check the label to be sure that natural sugars are involved. Simple syrup is also easy to make at home and you can be creative with seasonal flavors.

MASTER HOMEMADE SIMPLE SYRUP

IN A SMALL SAUCEPAN, COMBINE 1 CUP SUGAR WITH 1 CUP water. Simmer over medium heat, stirring, until the sugar dissolves completely. Sterilize (by boiling or running through the dishwasher) a capped bottle or lidded jar. Once the syrup has cooled, pour it into the bottle and store in the fridge for up to a month.

The same 1:1 ratio applies to agave nectar, and demerara and turbinado sugars, but honey is a 2:1 ratio with water. Rich simple syrup is also made at a 2:1 ratio of sugar to water.

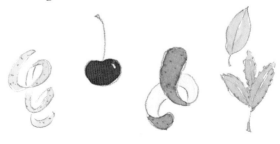

Flavored Simple Syrups

Flavor-infused simple syrups are sometimes specified in cocktails, but they also expand your flavor palate when creating custom concoctions (see page 182). Add a tablespoon of flavored syrup to a tall glass filled with ice and pour in sparkling water for a refreshing drink any time. Some infused syrups will keep for up to a month, but it's best to use them within 2 weeks.

Basil or Mint Simple Syrup: Add 1 cup picked leaves to the hot simple syrup and let steep off heat for 1 hour. Strain through a fine-mesh sieve, let cool, and bottle.

Bay Leaf Simple Syrup: Add 4 bay leaves (preferably Turkish) to the hot simple syrup and let steep off heat for 30 minutes. Strain through a fine-mesh sieve, let cool, and bottle.

Black Pepper Simple Syrup: Add 10 whole black peppercorns and 10 crushed black peppercorns to the hot simple syrup and let steep off heat for 30 minutes. Strain through a fine-mesh sieve, let cool, and bottle.

Cardamom Simple Syrup: Add 10 cardamom pods to the sugar and water and let boil for 8 minutes. Let steep off heat for 2 hours. Strain through a fine-mesh sieve, let cool, and bottle.

Cinnamon Simple Syrup: Add 2 cinnamon sticks to the sugar and water and simmer for 5 minutes. Let steep off heat for 8 hours. Strain through a fine-mesh sieve, let cool, and bottle.

Cucumber Simple Syrup: Add 1 cucumber (chopped, but not peeled) to the hot simple syrup and let steep off heat for 1 hour. Strain through a fine-mesh sieve, let cool, and bottle.

Fruit Simple Syrups: Add 1½ cups peeled fresh or frozen fruit (blueberry, cranberry, peach, raspberry, rhubarb, or strawberry) to the sugar and water. Simmer, stirring, for 25 minutes. Strain through a fine-mesh sieve, let cool, and bottle. For citrus fruit–flavored syrups, use 1½ cups freshly squeezed juice and proceed as above. For cranberries, reduce the cooking time to 15 minutes.

Ginger Simple Syrup: Add one (10-inch) knob of peeled ginger root, cut into small pieces, to the sugar and water and let boil for 10 minutes. Let steep off heat for 1 hour. Strain through a fine-mesh sieve, let cool, and bottle.

Jalapeño Simple Syrup: Add 1 jalapeño pepper (sliced lengthwise and seeded) to the hot simple syrup and let steep off heat for 1 hour or up to overnight. Strain through a fine-mesh sieve, let cool, and bottle.

Lavender Simple Syrup: Add 1 tablespoon food-grade lavender to the sugar and water and boil for 2 minutes. Remove from heat and let steep for 15 minutes. Strain through a fine-mesh sieve, let cool, and bottle.

Pomegranate Simple Syrup (Also Known as Grenadine): Replace the water with pomegranate juice, heating it over medium heat until it just begins to bubble (do not let it boil). Remove from the heat, add the sugar, and stir until it has dissolved. Stir in ¼ teaspoon fresh lemon juice and 2 to 3 drops of orange-flower water. Let cool and bottle.

Rose Simple Syrup: Reduce the water to ½ cup and dissolve sugar as directed. Remove from heat and stir in ½ cup food-grade rosewater. Let cool and bottle.

Tea Simple Syrup: Add 2 tablespoons Earl Grey, Lapsang souchong, or chai tea to the water and bring to a boil. Add the sugar and stir until dissolved. Strain through a fine-mesh sieve, let cool, and bottle.

Thyme Simple Syrup: Add 8 sprigs of fresh thyme to the sugar and water. Let steep off heat for 1 hour. Strain through a fine-mesh sieve, let cool, and bottle.

INFUSIONS

SPARKLING WATERS AND VARIOUS TYPES OF ALCOHOL ARE available in a variety of flavors, many of which are of questionable quality. As with simple syrups (see page 20), it's easy to make infusions at home—and in the case of alcohol, a lot more practical. Why buy a large bottle of lemon-flavored vodka when you can make a small amount at home that will taste much better?

Infused Alcohol

Add about ½ cup of your infusing ingredients to a lidded pint container and muddle with a wooden spoon. Fill the container with the alcohol of your choice, cover the container, and shake well. Put the container aside for 1 to 7 days, shaking once each day. The more intense the flavor of your infusing ingredient, the less time spent in the jar, so taste a sample often. For example, jalapeños should be ready in a few hours, while spices and herbs will take 3 to 4 days. Fruit, citrus zests, and food-grade florals should be left for 1 week.

It's often suggested that only a neutral spirit like vodka be used for infusions, but why limit yourself? Tequila will be complemented by pepper and spice, while bourbon likes peaches, orange zest, cherry, and rich spices like cardamom. Gin is made from a variety of botanicals and the flavor varies widely (especially in small-batch bottles), so try some classic combinations like cucumber or lime to start. If you're not sure about your choices, use smaller amounts to experiment.

Infused Water

If you have a home-soda machine (like a SodaStream), use your simple syrups to make customized sparkling water. Or infuse still water in a pitcher in the fridge overnight. Drink it straight or make it the base for carbonation. Citrus fruit, berries, cucumbers, mint, fresh ginger, vanilla bean—you're only limited here by what flavors you like to drink.

GO AHEAD, BE BITTER

A DASH OF BITTERS IS THE FINAL TOUCH TO MANY A COCKTAIL. Like your favorite hot sauce, just a few drops can have a big impact on the overall flavor. In common with many liqueurs, some of the most famous bitters were developed as patent medicines and digestive aids. These tiny bottles of base alcohol infused with a proprietary blend of herbs, barks, roots, and other botanicals go back to ancient times, but first gained popularity in the United States in the early 1800s. Although most bitters production ended with Prohibition, a few of the companies survived and continue to be among today's best-selling brands. Bitters are where the best craft cocktail bartenders let their imaginations run wild, and bars across the country now offer a variety of housemade blends. There are also hundreds of small-batch bitters made locally everywhere. Here are some brands you should know.

Angostura is a brand of aromatic bitters, developed in the town of Angostura, Venezuela, and now made in Trinidad and Tobago. The super-secret recipe dates back to 1824. This is the most popular type of bitters, specified in an Old-Fashioned, a Manhattan (page 52), and a Champagne cocktail, among many others.

Peychaud's Bitters was created in 1830 in a New Orleans pharmacy and is the bitters of choice when making a Sazerac cocktail (see page 76). It is lighter and slightly sweeter than Angostura. Peychaud's is now owned by the Sazerac company, which also produces Regans' Orange Bitters No. 6, developed by famed bartender Gaz Regan in the early 1990s.

Fee Brothers has been selling liquor in Rochester, New York, since the mid-1800s (they survived Prohibition by selling altar wine) and produce a full line of bitters in flavors ranging from Aztec Chocolate to West Indian Orange.

Hella Bitters, of Brooklyn, New York, is one of the new bitters companies to rise out of the artisanal movement. In addition to an interesting range of flavors that includes Smoked Chili bitters, they also offer a "craft your own bitters" kit that comes with everything needed.

Serve It with a Twist, or Not

One downside of the farm-to-glass movement is that some bartenders want to include an entire garden in the cocktail. Specific garnishes are often part of a cocktail recipe, but otherwise, resist the temptation that every drink needs a cherry on top. Remember Coco Chanel's advice on accessories: "Before you leave the house, look in the mirror and take one thing off."

With a sharp paring knife or a peeler, you can easily create a citrus twist by peeling just the zest of a lemon, lime, or orange. A thin circular slice of lime is also attractive wedged to the side of a glass or floating on top of the drink. And sometimes a cherry actually can be just the thing that's needed.

How to Rim a Glass with Colored Sugar or Salt

Rimming a cocktail glass with sugar or salt enhances the taste of many drinks. You can add more drama by dying the sugar to match the cocktail or the season. Pour 1/2 cup superfine sugar (or use regular granulated sugar if that's what you have on hand) into a clean, lidded pint container. Add up to 6 drops of food coloring in the shade of your choice. Cover with the lid and shake vigorously until the color is evenly distributed. Store the sugar in a dry place; it will keep for months.

To rim the glass, pour the sugar onto a small plate (that's wider than the rim of your glass) and spread it across the surface. Rub a wedge of lime around the rim of the glass to moisten the edge, turn the cocktail glass over, and dip the rim firmly into the sugar. Tap the glass gently to remove any excess. The rimming method is the same for salt.

Here's
What
We're
Drinking

Sparkling New Year

SEE THE NEW YEAR IN WITH A LOT OF SPARKLE.
Even if you've broken the budget with holiday shopping, a
bubbly toast at New Year's is not out of reach. The most
famous drink to come out of Harry's Bar in Venice is surely
the Bellini, a beautiful seasonal combination of white peaches
and Prosecco, Champagne's more affordable Italian cousin
(see page 31). It's less well known that the Bellini has some
very colorful friends, all named for Italian artists and com-
posers, that make for a very colorful and sparkling bar setup.
Consider channeling Cher in *Moonstruck* and add a little
Italian opera to your playlist for the evening.

Felice Anno Nuovo!
(Happy New Year!)

HARRY'S HOLIDAY BAR

MAKES 15 TO 20 SERVINGS

*It is said that the Bellini got its name because the color
reminded Harry's Bar owner Giuseppe Cipriani of a painting
by the Italian artist Giovanni Bellini. Similarly inspired cocktails
soon followed: the Puccini (made with mandarin orange), named
for the composer of La Bohème; the Rossini (strawberries), for
the composer of The Barber of Seville; and the Tintoretto (pomegranate), named for the Italian painter and the most fun to say.*

*While the original Bellini is made from a puree of white peaches,
they are hard to find even when in season. This recipe uses peach nectar.
To add to the variety of flavors, consider adding acai berry, raspberry,
mango, or even blueberry puree to your selection. Simply combine
1 (16-ounce) bag of frozen fruit with 1 tablespoon agave
nectar and 1 cup of water in a blender and pulse until smooth.
Name after your favorite Italian artist or composer.*

*Before serving, pour each juice or puree into glass pitchers,
with the corresponding garnishes in small bowls.
Keep the Prosecco on ice alongside.*

FOR THE BELLINI

1 ounce peach nectar

3 ounces Prosecco

Lime twist, for garnish

FOR THE PUCCINI

**1 ounce freshly squeezed
mandarin orange juice**

3 ounces Prosecco

Orange twist, for garnish

FOR THE ROSSINI

1 ounce strawberry puree

3 ounces Prosecco

Fresh strawberry slice, for garnish

FOR THE TINTORETTO

1 ounce pomegranate juice

3 ounces Prosecco

3 pomegranate seeds, for garnish

Pour the fruit juice or puree into a chilled Champagne flute and top with the Prosecco. Add the corresponding garnish to the flute.

Serve with . . .
PUFF PASTRY TREATS

A package of store-bought puff pastry kept in the freezer is a hostess's best friend and can form the basis for any number of snacks and hors d'oeuvres. Here are four suggestions.

ARTICHOKE DIP SQUARES

MAKES 10 PIECES

Preheat the oven to 375°F. Thaw 2 sheets of frozen puff pastry and press them into a 15x10-inch (jelly roll) pan. Press the dough 1 inch up the side of the pan. Bake until light golden brown, 10 to 12 minutes. Meanwhile, in a medium bowl, mix together 1 (14-ounce) can artichoke hearts, drained and chopped; 1 (9-ounce) box frozen chopped spinach, thawed and squeezed to drain all the liquid; ¾ cup Parmesan cheese; ⅔ cup mayonnaise; ⅔ cup sour cream; 1 teaspoon garlic powder; 1 teaspoon onion powder; and a dash of hot sauce. Spread the mixture evenly over the baked crust and sprinkle the top with 2 cups shredded sharp cheddar cheese. Reduce the oven temperature to 350°F and bake until the filling is hot and bubbly and the cheese has melted, 8 to 10 minutes. Cut into 1½-inch squares and serve warm.

FIG AND BRIE HAND PIES

Preheat the oven to 375°F. Thaw 2 sheets of frozen puff pastry. Unfold the puff pastry and cut into thirds lengthwise (use the creases as your guide). Cut each panel into 4 pieces (2¼-inch tall x 3 inches wide); you'll have 12 rectangles from each sheet. Slice 12 small slivers (with the rind) from half a wedge of cold Brie (about 4 ounces). Beat 1 large egg with 1 tablespoon of milk and brush half the rectangles. Place a piece of cheese on each. Top the cheese with 1 teaspoon of fig preserves (you'll need about ⅓ cup total). Place another rectangle of pastry dough on top and seal the edges firmly with a fork. Prick the top lightly. Place on a parchment-lined baking sheet, brush the tops with more egg wash and sprinkle with sea salt. Bake until golden brown, 12 to 14 minutes. Let cool slightly before serving.

MUSHROOM TARTLETS

MAKES 20 PIECES

Preheat the oven to 400°F. Thaw 1 sheet of frozen puff pastry. In a sauté pan, melt 2 tablespoons of butter. Add ½ pound fresh mushrooms, finely diced, and ½ cup finely diced onion. Sauté until soft, about 8 minutes. Season with ⅛ teaspoon cayenne pepper, 1 teaspoon fresh thyme, 1 tablespoon fresh lemon juice, ½ teaspoon salt, and a few grinds of black pepper. In a small bowl, mix together 1 tablespoon all-purpose flour and ½ cup half-and-half. Stir the flour mixture into the mushrooms. Stir until the mixture thickens.

Unfold the pastry sheet on a lightly floured surface and roll into a 15x12-inch rectangle. Cut into 20 (3-inch) squares. Press the squares into 20 (1½-inch) mini muffin-pan cups. Place about 1 tablespoon filling into each square. Sprinkle with grated Parmesan cheese. Bake until the pastry is golden brown, about 15 minutes. Let the pastries cool in the pan on a wire rack for 10 minutes. Sprinkle with parsley before serving.

BACON AND EGG TARTLETS

MAKES 20 PIECES

Preheat the oven to 400°F. Thaw 1 sheet of frozen puff pastry. Lay 10 slices of bacon on a rack inside a rimmed baking sheet and bake at 400°F until crispy, 15 to 20 minutes. Remove to paper towels to drain. In a mixing bowl, whisk 6 large eggs together with 4 tablespoons water, salt, and freshly ground pepper.

Prepare the puff pastry tart shells as described for the Mushroom Tartlets opposite. Spoon the egg mixture into the pastry shells and bake at 400°F until the pastry is golden and the eggs are puffy and set, about 15 minutes. Top the tarts with a shard of crisp bacon and sprinkle with chopped chives.

In the Netflix Queue

WHEN THE HOLIDAYS END AND THE COLD WEATHER sets in, it's time to spend some quality time with your couch and the TV shows and movies that have been piling up in your Netflix queue. You can even invite over a friend. Great series lend themselves to custom cocktails—you might want to invent your own, inspired by your favorite binge watching (see page 184). Here are a few to get you started, with a big bowl of popcorn (see page 42) on the side.

THE STARS HOLLOW

*While Luke's Diner provides the Gilmore girls' hometown
with its morning jolt of java, this might be the cocktail that's
sipped by guests in the afternoon at the Dragonfly Inn, right
before enjoying one of Sookie's fabulous dinners. To up the coffee
flavor, use a vodka infused with espresso beans. For the coffee liqueur,
instead of the standard Kahlúa, try one of the fine artisanal brands
like Firelit or Bittermens New Orleans Coffee Liqueur.*

1¹/₂ ounces vodka

¹/₂ ounce anisette

¹/₂ ounce coffee liqueur

Lemon peel, to garnish

Fill a cocktail pitcher three-quarters full of ice. Add the vodka and
anisette and stir. Strain into a cocktail glass and float the liqueur on
top. Garnish with a twist of lemon.

MOTHER OF DRAGONS

*Calling all Khaleesi to play a game of thrones.
When the Silver Queen Daenerys has accounted for all her
dragons, she might just curl up with this cocktail, a slightly spicy
mixture that may have you breathing some fire of your own.*

2 ounces gin

1 ounce green chartreuse

¹/₂ ounce jalapeño simple syrup (page 22)

¹/₂ ounce freshly squeezed lime juice

2 ounces sparkling water

Dragon fruit slice, for garnish

Fill a shaker three-quarters full with ice. Add the gin, chartreuse, syrup, and lime juice. Shake well and strain over ice into a highball glass and top with the sparkling water. Garnish with a slice of dragon fruit, if you dare.

CRAZY EYES

*If orange is the new black, you might need some new accessories.
Smoky and rich, this is a cocktail that will calm any anxiety.*

2 ounces mezcal

¹/₂ ounce Cointreau

¹/₂ ounce brandy

¹/₂ ounce Amaretto

¹/₂ ounce freshly squeezed lime juice

Orange peel, for garnish

Fill a shaker three-quarters full with ice. Add the mezcal, Cointreau, brandy, Amaretto, and lime juice. Shake and pour over ice into a rocks glass. Garnish with a twist of orange peel.

FRANKLY BITTER

Oh, Mr. Underwood, you leave so many bitter enemies in your wake, it's a wonder that your house of cards hasn't collapsed. Although Frank drinks his bourbon neat, this cocktail gets an extra dose of bitter flavors and a hint of peach in tribute to his South Carolina hometown.

2 ounces bourbon

³/₄ ounce Aperol

1 ounce peach nectar

Dash of orange bitters

Fresh peach wedge, for garnish

Fill a shaker three-quarters full with ice. Add the bourbon, Aperol, peach nectar, and bitters. Shake and pour over ice into a rocks glass. Garnish with a wedge of fresh peach, if desired.

Serve with . . .
DIY MICROWAVE POPCORN

*Yes, you really can avoid all the salt and
artificial flavors by making your own microwave popcorn—
and all you need is a paper bag.*

Makes about 10 cups

Place ¹/₂ cup popcorn kernels in a brown paper lunch bag. Fold the top of the bag down three times, making sure to leave room in the bag for the popped kernels. (DO NOT staple the bag closed!) Set the bag on its side in the microwave and microwave on HIGH for 2 minutes. Don't leave the kitchen—the timing all depends on the power of your microwave. When the popping slows down to about 5 seconds between pops, turn off the microwave. Open the bag with care and pour the popcorn into a large bowl. Sprinkle with ¼ teaspoon popcorn salt (see Note).

Note: Popcorn salt is simply a finer grade of salt. To make your own, grind a few tablespoons of kosher salt in your coffee grinder.

How to Make Flavored Popcorn

If you want to add flavorings, toss the popped popcorn with melted butter or olive oil; that will help any seasoning to stick better. Start with about 1 tablespoon of seasoning and increase according to your preference. Here are some suggestions to try.

Nutritional Yeast (like Bragg's): Sounds awful, but sprinkling this on top gives popcorn a great cheesy taste.

Ranch: Melt 2½ tablespoons butter and mix with 1 ounce ranch seasoning mix. Toss with 1 tablespoon chopped chives.

Garlic-Herb Butter: Melt 2 tablespoons butter and mix with ½ teaspoon garlic powder and ½ teaspoon each of finely chopped fresh rosemary, sage, and thyme, or whatever herbs you like.

Gruyère-Porcini: Pulse ⅓ cup dried porcini mushrooms in a coffee grinder. Toss the popcorn with 3 tablespoons melted butter, then toss with the mushroom powder and ¾ cup finely grated Gruyère cheese.

Wasabi: Make a paste of 2 teaspoons each wasabi powder and water and ½ teaspoon salt. Add to 3 tablespoons melted butter and blend well. Drizzle over the popcorn and toss.

Sriracha-Lime: Add 2 tablespoons sriracha and 2 teaspoons lime juice with 3 tablespoons melted butter. Toss with the popcorn and sprinkle with finely grated lime zest.

Barbecue: Combine 2 teaspoons garlic salt, 1½ teaspoons each smoked paprika and sugar, 1 teaspoon each of onion and chili powder, ½ teaspoon salt, and ¼ teaspoon ground mustard with 3 tablespoons melted butter and toss with the popcorn.

Cinnamon Sugar: Mix together ⅓ cup sugar, 2 teaspoons cinnamon, and 1 teaspoon kosher salt. Toss the popcorn with 3 tablespoons melted butter, then toss again with the cinnamon sugar.

Game Day

WHY NOT GATHER FRIENDS AROUND YOUR HOME screen instead of heading down to the local sports bar for the big game? It's guaranteed to be more fun and a lot more comfortable. Beer is the order of the day and beer cocktails are a great way to show you're not in college anymore. Make up a big batch of chili (see page 48) and keep it warm in the slow cooker to feed the crowd.

BLACK VELVET

This dramatically beautiful cocktail is said to have been created in London in memory of Queen Victoria's husband, Prince Albert. Guinness is the traditional choice for this drink, but a local craft stout is a great substitute. Because the stout and the sparkling wine remain layered, it is very effective to serve this in a Champagne flute.

4 ounces chilled brut sparkling wine

4 ounces chilled stout

Brandied cherry (see page 56), for garnish

Pour the sparkling wine into a chilled Champagne flute or cocktail glass. Add the stout beer, but do not stir. Drop a brandied cherry in the glass.

CAMPARI SHANDY

Shandies come in many types and flavors.
Traditionally a mix of beer and a soft drink, they can
also incorporate lemonade, fruit juices, or even hard ciders.
This modern and refreshing take comes from a recipe that Orangette
blogger Molly Wizenberg and her husband, Brandon Pettit,
owners of the Seattle restaurants Delancey and Essex,
shared with the Food52 community.

2 ounces Campari
12 ounces cold, light-colored beer
1 lime wedge

Pour the Campari into a tall chilled glass. Add the beer and stir to mix. Squeeze the lime wedge into the glass, and then drop the wedge in.

Serve with . . .
THREE-BEAN CHILI

Chili is a satisfying meal that you can fix and then forget. Choose a vegetarian option that will please carnivores, too, and purchase corn bread to serve warm on the side.

SERVES 4 TO 6

Heat 2 tablespoons olive oil in a large heavy pot over medium heat. Add 1 medium chopped onion, 1 large seeded and chopped red and green bell pepper, 1 large seeded and chopped jalapeño pepper, and 4 cloves of garlic, crushed and chopped. Sauté until the vegetables soften, 3 to 5 minutes. Pour in 1 cup light-colored beer and add 1 (32-ounce) can crushed tomatoes, and 1 (14-ounce) can each of black beans, red kidney beans, and chickpeas. Stir to combine. Season the chili with 2 tablespoons chili powder, 1 tablespoon ground cumin, 1 tablespoon hot sauce, and salt and freshly ground black pepper. Let simmer for 1 hour, taste, and adjust seasoning. Transfer to a slow cooker, if you like, to keep warm for serving.

Place toppings—chopped onions, shredded cheddar cheese, sour cream, and sliced jalapeños—in small bowls alongside.

New York City Nights

BRIGHT LIGHTS, BIG CITY. WHETHER SIPPING A Manhattan in an upscale hotel bar or testing the latest molecular mixology in artisanal Brooklyn, the Big Apple has some major bona fides when it comes to cocktails. Here's a city that melds many cultures, and the cocktails it's known for are as direct and upfront as the people who live there.

THE MANHATTAN

Simply perfection, just like the borough itself. It's said that many a Wall Street broker ends the trading day just as the millionaire J. P. Morgan did, with a Manhattan. Served straight up or on the rocks, this rich-tasting, warming cocktail is perfect for sipping. Don't skip the cherries. They provide a perfectly sweet balance to the rye.

2 ounces rye whiskey

1 ounce sweet vermouth

2 dashes Angostura bitters

Brandied cherry (see page 56), for garnish

Fill a cocktail pitcher three-quarters full of ice. Add the rye, vermouth, and bitters, and stir. Strain into a chilled cocktail glass and garnish with a brandied cherry.

NEW YORK COCKTAIL

*Just as Manhattan often overshadows the other boroughs,
the New York cocktail has lived in the shadow of its more famous
sister drink. Both the Manhattan and the New York will
benefit from a quality American rye, and any of the artisanal,
small-batch blends are a good choice here.*

2 ounces rye whiskey
³/₄ ounce freshly squeezed lime juice
¹/₂ ounce simple syrup
1 teaspoon Grenadine (see page 22)
Orange peel, for garnish

In a shaker filled three-quarters full with ice, add the rye, lime
juice, simple syrup, and Grenadine. Shake and strain into an iced-
filled cocktail glass. Garnish with a twist of orange.

THE COSMOPOLITAN

*"Why did we ever stop drinking these?" asked
Miranda, in* Sex and the City. *"Because everyone else
started," Samantha replied. Sometimes a great cocktail can
become a victim of its own popularity, especially in the age of artisanal
cocktails, when everyone is looking for something new. But there's
a reason that the Cosmo is considered a modern classic. One sip and
you'll wonder why you ever stopped drinking it, too.*

2 ounces vodka
³/₄ ounce Cointreau
³/₄ ounce freshly squeezed lime juice
¹/₂ ounce cranberry juice
¹/₂ ounce simple syrup
Orange peel, for garnish

To a shaker filled three-quarters full with ice, add the vodka,
Cointreau, lime juice, cranberry juice, and simple syrup. Shake and
strain into a chilled cocktail glass. Garnish with a twist of orange
peel, if desired.

Serve with ...

NEW YORK CITY FLATBREADS

Sure, New York's known for its pizza,
but using store-bought flatbreads are an easy way to
feature a variety of the city's classic flavors.

Purchase sheets of the Middle Eastern flatbread lavash (Trader Joe's makes a good one). Preheat the oven to 375°F. Warm the lavash until golden brown, 5 to 6 minutes. Top with: sliced steak, crumbled blue cheese and baby arugula; roasted tomatoes and Parmesan cheese; cream cheese, sprinkled with everything bagel seasoning and topped with thin slices of smoked salmon and a garnish of fresh dill; or a thin layer of sauerkraut topped with thin-sliced corned beef and dot with Russian dressing. Slice into squares.

BRANDIED CHERRIES

We've become accustomed to store-bought cocktail cherries that are so sweet they're almost candy, but you'll now find good-quality jars available from some of the artisanal bitters makers. It's very easy to make them at home, too. Customize this basic recipe with your favorite spices; bourbon and/or rum can also be added to or substituted for the brandy. You can choose not to stem and pit the cherries, but you may want to trim the stems a bit if you leave them intact; they'll look prettier.

Stem and pit 1 pound of cherries and set them aside. In a saucepan, combine ½ cup sugar, ½ cup water, 2 tablespoons lemon juice, 1 stick cinnamon, ¼ teaspoon freshly ground nutmeg, 1 vanilla bean, and a pinch of salt. Cook, stirring frequently, until the sugar is dissolved and the mixture thickens, about 10 minutes. Remove the pan from the heat and stir in 1 cup of brandy. Add the cherries and stir to coat. Let cool completely and transfer to a sterilized 1-quart lidded jar. Store in the refrigerator and let macerate for 8 weeks before using. The cherries will keep, refrigerated, for up to 1 year.

Five Boroughs of Cocktails

We all know the Manhattan, but there's actually a cocktail named for each of New York City's five boroughs. Two are variations on a classic Martini (page 66): the Bronx Cocktail adds orange juice, while the Queens adds pineapple juice. A Brooklyn cocktail blends rye, vermouth, maraschino liqueur, and Amer Picon, while the city's southernmost borough picks up a tropical theme: the Staten Island Ferry mixes equal parts Malibu rum and pineapple juice over ice.

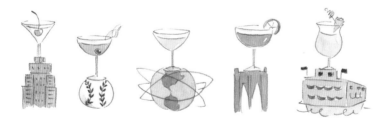

Ice-Skating Party

WINTER WINDS CALL FOR COCKTAILS THAT WILL warm you to the bottom of your toes. Whether you've gathered with friends at the local rink or rented a ski lodge for the weekend, this pair of cocktails will serve both the sophisticated palate and the sweet tooth. These occasions are just made for sharing fondue (see page 62)—if you don't have a fondue pot, it's a safe bet you'll find one in your grandmother's attic.

BOULEVARDIER

*Replacing a Negroni's gin with bourbon, this cocktail
made its debut in 1927's* Barflies and Cocktails *and is said
to have been named for a Parisian literary magazine of the same
name. It's perfect for sipping in front of a roaring fire.*

2 ounces bourbon

³/₄ ounce Campari

³/₄ ounce sweet vermouth

Brandied cherry (page 56), for garnish

Fill a mixing glass or small pitcher halfway with ice. Add the
bourbon, Campari, and vermouth and stir gently. Strain into an
ice-filled rocks glass and garnish with the cherry.

THE IRISH ITALIAN

This is a luxurious and very boozy hot chocolate, made with Italy's famous hazelnut-chocolate spread Nutella. A further nutty note comes from the almond-flavored Amaretto, while Baileys brings Irish whiskey and even more chocolate to the cup.

8 ounces whole milk

6 tablespoons Nutella

1 ounce heavy cream

1¹/₂ ounces Baileys Original Irish Cream

1 ounce Amaretto

Whipped cream for topping, optional

In a small saucepan over medium heat, combine the milk, Nutella, and cream. Whisk until the Nutella has melted and is completely incorporated. Reduce the heat to low, add the Baileys and Amaretto, and stir to combine. Heat until the mixture is hot, but do not let it boil. Remove from the heat, pour into tall heatproof mugs, and top with whipped cream, if desired.

Serve with . . .

Fondue, anyone? This pot of molten deliciousness never really goes out of style—we're talking melted cheese and chocolate, after all. Make one or both; each will pair well with winter cocktails.

CHOCOLATE FONDUE

SERVES 4

In a medium saucepan, combine 1¼ cups cream, 1 teaspoon pure vanilla extract, and 2 tablespoons butter. Bring to a simmer over medium heat. Remove from the heat and add 6 ounces each of both bittersweet and milk chocolate, broken into small pieces. Stir until completely melted and smooth. Transfer to a fondue pot set over a flame. Serve with strawberries, orange sections, and cubes of pound cake for dipping.

CLASSIC CHEESE FONDUE

Serves 6

Rub the inside of a 4-quart heavy pot with the cut sides of a halved garlic clove. Discard the garlic and add 1½ cups dry white wine to the pot. Bring the wine to a simmer over medium heat. Slowly add ½ pound each of coarsely grated Emmental and Gruyère cheese (about 2 cups each) to the wine and cook, stirring constantly, until the cheese is just melted. Be sure to stir in a zigzag rather than a circular motion so the cheese will melt smoothly. In a small bowl, whisk together 1 tablespoon cornstarch and 2 teaspoons brandy and stir it into the fondue. Bring the fondue to a simmer and cook, stirring until thickened, 5 to 8 minutes. Transfer the cheese mixture to a fondue pot set over a flame and sprinkle the top lightly with cayenne pepper. Serve with cubes of hearty white and brown bread, apple and pear slices, and grapes.

Martinis All Around

PERHAPS THE MOST FAMOUS OF ALL COCKTAILS, the Martini is made with gin, not vodka. Origin stories abound, as similar versions of the cocktail first began to appear in the early 1800s, but the Martini really came into its own during Prohibition, when gin (of the bathtub variety) was often the only liquor available. Today, the Martini has almost become a cocktail genre unto itself, with variations ranging from sweet to herbal to sour—along with a few made with vodka.

THE CLASSIC MARTINI

This is the recipe that appeared in
Frank Newman's American Bar, *published in 1904.*

3 ounces Plymouth gin

1 ounce dry vermouth

3 olives speared on a toothpick,
or a lemon twist, for garnish

Fill a cocktail pitcher three-quarters full with ice. Add the gin and vermouth and stir. Strain into a chilled cocktail glass. Garnish with 3 olives or a lemon twist.

Variations

DIRTY MARTINI

Add ¼ ounce of pickle brine (from the jar).

THE GIBSON

Substitute a pearl onion for the olive garnish.

THE VODKA MARTINI

*Cocktail expert and historian Dave Wondrich tells us
this drink was once called a Kangaroo (for reasons lost
to history) and then a Vodkatini. It's definitely a child of the
1950s, when vodka suddenly became all the rage. It's also
the basis for the most popular Martini variations.*

**3 ounces vodka
1 teaspoon vermouth
3 olives speared on a toothpick,
or a lemon twist, for garnish**

Fill a cocktail pitcher three-quarters full with ice. Add the gin and
vermouth and stir. Strain into a chilled cocktail glass. Garnish with
3 olives or a lemon twist.

Variations

The Apple-tini: In a shaker filled three-quarters full of ice, combine
1¹/₂ ounces vodka, ³/₄ ounce each apple brandy and apple juice, and
¹/₂ ounce freshly squeezed lime juice. Shake and strain into a chilled
cocktail glass. Garnish with an apple slice, if desired.

The Chocolate-tini: In a shaker filled three-quarters full of ice,
combine 2 ounces vodka, 1 ounce white crème de cacao, and ¹/₄ ounce
Cointreau. Shake and strain into a chilled cocktail glass. Pour in 1 ounce
Kahlúa and garnish with a cherry.

THE VESPER

What James Bond famously ordered in Casino Royale *was, in fact, a Vesper, taking its name from Vesper Lynd, the "Bond Girl" of Ian Fleming's first 007 novel. The Kina Lillet referenced in the book is today available under the label of Lillet Blanc, a fortified wine.*

2¹⁄₄ ounces dry gin

³⁄₄ ounce vodka

¹⁄₂ ounce Lillet Blanc

Lemon peel, for garnish

To a cocktail shaker filled three-quarters full with ice, add the gin, vodka, and Lillet. Shake and strain into a chilled cocktail glass. Garnish with a twist of lemon peel.

You Got This

WE ALL HAVE THOSE DAYS. WHETHER IT'S A BLOWUP
with a significant other, a fight with a friend, or maybe just a really bad day at the office, sometimes the perfect cocktail can bring the wisp of a smile to your face as you dry your tears—and remember, there's always chocolate cake (see page 73).

THE BLUE MONDAY

*This slightly bitter, citrus-y cocktail will transport you to a
Caribbean beach. Curaçao, from the island of the same name, is a
liqueur flavored with the aromatic dried peels of laraha citrus, a fruit
that is similar to the Valencia orange. The blue comes from food coloring.*

2 ounces vodka

1 ounce Cointreau

¹/₂ ounce blue Curaçao

Fill a cocktail pitcher three-quarters full with ice. Add the vodka,
Cointreau, and blue Curaçao, and stir. Strain into a chilled cocktail glass.

THE SIMPLE TREUSE

*Sometimes we all have to face simple truths, but this delicious
cocktail, created by Detroit bartender Tiffanie Dyer, can ease the mind
of any worries. To double-strain, pour the drink holding a small, fine
strainer (like a tea strainer) between the shaker and the glass.*

1 orange wedge

1 ounce rye whiskey, preferably Rittenhouse

³/₄ ounce freshly squeezed lemon juice

³/₄ ounce Aperol

³/₄ ounce yellow chartreuse

Add the ingredients to a cocktail shaker. Muddle the orange a few times and fill the shaker two thirds full with ice. Shake well and double strain into a cocktail glass.

Serve with ...

For those days when you just want some chocolaty deliciousness right now, here is a single-serving cake made in a mug in the microwave. It tastes way better than you'd ever imagine.

FIVE-MINUTE CHOCOLATE CAKE

Serves 1

In a large, microwave-safe mug, mix together 4 tablespoons each of flour and sugar and 2 tablespoons cocoa powder (do not use hot chocolate mix). Add 1 egg and mix completely. Add 3 tablespoons each of milk and olive oil. Add 3 tablespoons of melted chocolate (you can do this in the microwave, too) and a splash of pure vanilla extract and mix again. Put the cup in the microwave and zap it on HIGH for about 3 minutes. The cake will rise over the top of the mug, but don't worry, it won't spill out. Let the cake cool a little, then tip out onto a plate, if desired. Who are we kidding? Just grab a spoon and eat it straight out of the mug.

Mardi Gras

LAISSEZ LES BONS TEMPS ROULER! THERE'S NO better party city than New Orleans and there's no bigger party than Mardi Gras. Held each year on Shrove Tuesday, Mardi Gras is one final day of excess before the sacrificial period of Lent begins. Parades, music, masks, and beads thrown from elaborate floats—try to catch as many as you can with the one hand that doesn't hold your drink. New Orleans is the birthplace of many elaborate cocktails that are well worth the effort of their mixology. Here are two of the city's classics.

SAZERAC

*Antoine Peychaud (of bitters fame, see page 25) first mixed
up the Sazerac in the late 1830s for friends who gathered after hours
in his French Quarter pharmacy. Its popularity spread throughout
the city and, eventually, the country. The original recipe used French
brandy instead of rye, and pastis replaced absinthe when the latter was
illegal in the United States. You may substitute bourbon for the rye, if
you wish; you may not use any other brand of bitters but Peychaud's.*

1 sugar cube

3 dashes Peychaud's bitters

1¹/₂ ounces rye whiskey

¹/₄ ounce absinthe

Lemon peel, for garnish

Fill a rocks glass with ice. Place the sugar cube in a second
rocks glass and add the bitters. Use a small wooden spoon to crush
the sugar cube, then add the rye. Empty the ice from the first
glass and add the absinthe. Swirl to coat the glass, then discard the remaining absinthe. Pour the rye mixture into the
absinthe-coated glass and garnish with a twist of lemon peel.

RAMOS GIN FIZZ

*Also called the New Orleans Fizz, the drink was created in
1888 by Henry Ramos, owner of the Imperial Cabinet Saloon. Because
the drink requires a long shaking time to properly emulsify the cream
and the egg white, it's said that the shaker was passed from bartender to
bartender until it reached the end of the saloon bar. It's essential to shake
for the full time—wrap the shaker in a kitchen towel to keep your hands
from getting too cold. Most recipes don't call for garnish, but a cherry
looks very pretty set against the pale, creamy cocktail.*

2 ounces dry gin

1 ounce heavy cream

1/2 ounce simple syrup

1/2 ounce freshly squeezed lemon juice

2 teaspoons superfine sugar

1 egg white

3 or 4 drops of orange flower water

1 ounce sparkling water

Cherry, for garnish

Combine the gin, cream, simple syrup, lemon juice, sugar, egg
white, and orange flower water in a shaker and shake vigorously
for 30 seconds. Add ice and shake vigorously again for 2 minutes
more. Strain into a chilled cocktail glass and top with the
sparkling water. Stir very briefly and top with a cherry, if desired.

THE HURRICANE

*You can still order a Hurricane at its birthplace,
Pat O'Brien's bar in the French Quarter, and it will be served
in the tall, curved glass that shares its name. This drink is a bit on the
sweet side, so be sure to use fresh lime juice for a good flavor balance.*

1 ounce light rum

1 ounce dark rum

¹/₂ ounce Grenadine, or passion fruit syrup

1 ounce freshly squeezed orange juice

¹/₂ ounce freshly squeezed lime juice

¹/₂ teaspoon superfine sugar, or more, to taste

Orange slice, for garnish

Cherry, for garnish

Fill a shaker three-quarters full with ice. Add the light and dark rum, Grenadine, orange and lime juices, and sugar. Shake and pour into a rocks glass (or a hurricane glass, if you have one). Garnish with a slice of orange and a cherry.

Serve with . . .
ANDOUILLE SAUSAGE BITES

*New Orleans is well known for its spicy food,
and spice will pair well with cocktails that are on the sweet
side. Andouille is a pork sausage seasoned with cayenne, paprika,
sage, and other herbs and spices. It's a favorite of Cajun cuisine.
This simple appetizer recipe calls for andouille sausage links,
but you can substitute a chicken version, if you prefer.*

SERVES 6 TO 8

Cut 1 pound andouille sausage links into 1-inch slices. Spray a large sauté pan with nonstick cooking spray, add the sausage pieces, and brown on all sides. Place the sausage on paper towels to drain and serve while still warm on a platter with toothpicks and a bowl of (preferably Creole) mustard for dipping.

London Calling

POSH PRIVATE CLUBS, TOTALLY HIP UPSCALE BARS, or elegant weekend lawn parties at country estates—cocktails in London are a far cry from having a pint down at the pub. If there's one liquor that's quintessentially British, it's gin. And in this time of artisanal mixology, gin, with its botanical profile, has been enjoying a renaissance, especially in London (where it never *really* went out of style). Whether you're settling in for the finals at Wimbledon or celebrating victory in a game of croquet, a gin-based drink is the hallmark of any summer activity.

GIN AND TONIC

Gin was first designed for medicinal purposes, and the
"G&T" even more so. British troops in India in the early 1800s
hoped to ward off malaria by mixing quinine (an extract of cinchona
bark, see page 20) into their water. Soon they added gin, and just a
touch of sugar (to make the medicine go down). The troops brought
the drink home to England, and its popularity has never waned. The
G&T is a simple drink, which makes the quality of the ingredients
more important. Choose a good dry-style gin (see Types of Gin, page
85) and a tonic water made from natural sugars (see page 20).

2 ounces dry gin
3 to 4 ounces cold tonic water
Wedge of lime

Fill a highball glass with ice. Add the gin, top off with tonic water, squeeze the lime wedge over and stir. Drop the lime wedge in the glass.

LAST DAYS OF THE RAJ

*This is a pretty and aromatic drink, nostalgic for the time
when India was the jewel in the crown of the British Empire.*

1¹/₂ ounces gin
2 teaspoons cardamom simple syrup
(page 21)
1 teaspoon orange flower water
3 ounces sparkling water
1 round lime slice

Fill a shaker three-quarters full with ice. Add the gin, simple syrup,
and orange flower water. Shake well and strain over ice into a
highball glass. Top with sparkling water and garnish with the lime
slice.

SLOE GIN FIZZ

Sloe berry bushes line the hedgerows of the British countryside.
Barely edible on their own, sloe berries made a tasty liqueur when
marinated in gin and sugar. Sloe gin is sold commercially now, and
you can also find beach plum gin made from the American equivalent.
This sweet-tart cocktail is especially refreshing on a hot summer day.

1 ounce sloe gin

1 ounce gin

³/₄ ounce freshly squeezed lemon juice

¹/₄ ounce simple syrup

3 ounces sparkling water

Maraschino cherry for garnish

Fill a shaker three-quarters full with ice. Add the sloe gin, gin, lemon juice, and simple syrup to a shaker. Shake well and strain into a highball glass filled with ice. Top with the sparkling water, stir, and garnish with a cherry.

Types of Gin

Although all liquors have individual qualities and flavors that vary across brands, gin is actually divided into a number of different categories. A blend must contain juniper berries to be legally called gin, but additional botanicals will differ. Specific gin types are often listed as ingredients in some drink recipes, but nothing is set in stone. That said, many of the delicious gins being made by artisanal distillers will have more distinctive botanical flavor notes.

London Dry, or Dry Gin: The most common type, with strong notes of juniper. It is commonly recommended for martinis and gin and tonics.

Plymouth Gin: Less dry than London gin, with an earthier flavor. It must be made in Plymouth, England.

Old Tom Gin: A sweeter version of London dry gin. It is the gin of choice for a Tom Collins.

Genever, Holland, or Dutch Gin: Made from a malt grain base, which gives it a slightly darker color and a complex flavor that's closer to whiskey, while retaining the botanical essence.

New American, American, or International: Refers to the variety of gins being made by artisanal distillers. They're still gin, but with distinctive proprietary botanical blends.

Navy Strength: Gin that is bottled at 57 percent alcohol by volume (London style gin ranges between 40 and 45 percent). While rare, it is gaining popularity among distillers working in the New American style.

Serve with . . .
SHORTBREAD

Shortbread is so much more than Girl Scout cookies!
With a base made from just three ingredients, it makes a
great platform for both sweet and savory flavors, and the richness
of the biscuits are a perfect foil for the briskly botanical gin.

MAKES 24 PIECES

Preheat the oven to 300°F. With an electric mixer, cream together 1 cup softened butter and ½ cup sugar. Add 2½ cups flour and mix into a stiff dough. Press into an ungreased 9x13-inch baking pan, prick all over with a fork, and sprinkle with sugar. Bake until very lightly browned, 40 to 45 minutes. Let stand for 5 minutes, then cut into 24 squares while still warm, but leave in the pan until completely cool. (It will crisp as it cools.)

Variations

Lavender Shortbread: Add 1 to 3 teaspoons food-grade lavender to the dough.

Bacon Shortbread: Replace ¼ cup of the butter with bacon drippings and add 3 to 4 crumbled slices of crisp bacon to the dough.

Lemon-Thyme Shortbread: Add the zest of 1 lemon and 2 teaspoons fresh thyme leaves to the dough.

Chai Spice Shortbread: Add ⅛ teaspoon each ground cardamom and cinnamon, and a pinch of ground cloves and freshly ground black pepper to the dough.

Lemon-Chamomile Shortbread: Add the zest of 1 lemon and 1 teaspoon loose chamomile tea to the dough.

Cheddar Shortbread: Add 2 cups very finely grated cheddar cheese, ¾ teaspoon dry mustard, and ¼ teaspoon cayenne pepper to the dough.

Rosemary Shortbread: Add 2 tablespoons minced fresh rosemary leaves to the dough.

Curried Shortbread: Add 1 teaspoon curry powder, ½ teaspoon each of ground cumin and freshly ground black pepper, and ¼ teaspoon each ground turmeric and cayenne pepper to the dough.

Sunday Brunch Bloodies

WITHOUT A BLOODY MARY, CAN WE EVEN CALL it brunch? Most classic cocktails have their origins shrouded in myth, but it is widely accepted that the Bloody Mary as we know it today started out in Paris, but got its spice in New York. It's said that bartender Fernand Petiot developed the basic vodka and tomato mix in 1920s Paris at the famous Harry's New York Bar. After Prohibition, Petiot moved to New York and presided over the equally celebrated King Cole Bar at the St. Regis Hotel. It was there that horseradish, Tabasco sauce, lemon juice, and celery were added to the renamed Red Snapper, later taking back the name of the ruthless English queen.

THE BLOODY MARY

*Everyone tinkers with the classic recipe, adjusting the
spice to suit personal tastes. This one, adapted from the official
recipe of the King Cole Bar, makes a particularly spicy cocktail.
And as with most popular drinks, variations abound.
Some of the better choices are included here.*

2 to 4 ounces tomato juice

1 ounce vodka

1 teaspoon freshly squeezed lemon juice

3 dashes Worcestershire sauce

1/4 teaspoon fresh grated horseradish

1/4 teaspoon Tabasco sauce

1/4 teaspoon salt

1/4 teaspoon black pepper

1/4 teaspoon cayenne pepper

1 lemon wedge

1 celery stalk with leaves

Fill a shaker three-quarters full with ice. Add the tomato juice,
vodka, lemon juice, Worcestershire sauce, horseradish, Tabasco
sauce, and the salt and peppers. Shake well and strain into a large
glass filled with ice. Squeeze the lemon wedge into the glass and
drop it into the drink. Stir and garnish with the celery stalk.

Variations

The Bloody Maria: Substitute tequila for the vodka, finely chopped chili adobo for the horseradish, and jalapeño slices for the celery stalk.

The Bloody Caesar: Replace half the tomato juice with clam juice.

The Bloodless Mary: Not a virgin cocktail, but one made with tomato water instead of tomato juice.

Sriracha Bloody Mary: Replace the Tabasco sauce with sriracha.

Bloody Beet: Replace 1 ounce of the tomato juice with beet juice and add a strip of crisp bacon to the garnish.

Après Shopping

SHOPPING—HONESTLY, IT CAN JUST BE EXHAUSTING.
Whether you're fighting the crowds at a sample sale or searching for that perfect dress for next weekend's party, you'll definitely be needing a cocktail at the end of the day. Why not make one that's good for you, too? These drinks feature fresh juices and healing spices that will have you back scouring the racks in no time. Make up a big batch of snack mix (see page 96) for a protein-rich pick-me-up on the go.

THE ENERGIZER

Keep your eyes sharp for spotting bargains with this refreshing, slightly spicy, carrot juice cocktail. Spiced rum gives this drink a nice flavor, but regular rum works well, too. If you go with the latter, replace the ginger ale with the spicier ginger beer.

2 ounces spiced rum

1 ounce freshly squeezed carrot juice

$\frac{1}{2}$ ounce freshly squeezed lime juice

$\frac{1}{4}$ ounce ginger simple syrup (page 22)

Ginger ale

Sprig of fresh flat-leaf parsley, for garnish

Fill a shaker three-quarters full with ice. Add the spiced rum, carrot juice, lime juice, and ginger syrup. Shake well and pour into an ice-filled highball glass. Top with the ginger ale and garnish with a sprig of parsley.

GOLDEN GLOW

*Turmeric is said to have more health benefits than could
possibly be listed here, but this is a cocktail that will surely
cure any ills. As a bonus, it adds a gorgeous color, aroma,
and slightly bitter spice to this restorative drink.*

4 ounces mango juice

2 ounces bourbon

1 ounce black pepper simple syrup (page 21)

¹/₂ teaspoon turmeric powder

¹/₂ ounce freshly squeezed lemon juice

Fill a shaker three-quarters full with ice. Add the mango juice,
bourbon, black pepper syrup, turmeric, and lemon juice. Shake well
and strain over ice into a rocks glass.

Serve with . . .
SNACK MIX

*Snack mix is great to have on hand—you'll always have
something to serve when friends drop by unexpectedly.
Carry some in your bag while shopping for a quick energy bo
This is a "choose your own adventure" recipe—the final
combination of ingredients is up to you.*

Makes 8 to 10 cups

Preheat the oven to 250°F. In a large mixing bowl, combine
1 cup Chex cereal, 1 cup mini pretzels, 1 cup corn nuts, 1 cup
each of two kinds of unroasted nuts (almonds, cashews, peanuts,
or walnuts), 1 cup coconut flakes, ½ cup raw pepitas, and ½ cup
sunflower seeds. In a small saucepan, melt 6 tablespoons of butter.
Remove from the heat and stir in 2 tablespoons hot honey (or 1½
tablespoons regular honey and ½ tablespoon hot sauce), 1 teaspoon
each of cinnamon and ground ginger, and a pinch of salt. Pour
the seasoned butter over your cereal-nut mix and use a spoon to
toss well.

Spread the mixture in a single layer across 1 to 2 rimmed baking
sheets and bake, stirring occasionally, until dry and toasty, about 1
hour. Let the mix cool and, if desired, add 1 cup of dried cranberries
(or other dried fruit) and 1 cup of mini dark chocolate chips.
Store in an airtight container for up to 1 month.

Hosting Book Club

BOOK CLUBS ARE A REALLY GOOD EXCUSE TO get together with friends and sip cocktails, eat cheese— and maybe have a serious discussion about the book you've all just read. When it's your turn to host, don't panic. A pitcher filled with a wine-based cocktail or a cocktail with a literary bent pairs nicely with a cheese board that's easy to assemble (see page 102) and will keep the conversation flowing.

SANGARITA

Makes 8 servings

*Just as Sangria is a step up from regular wine, a
Sangarita is made even more special by the addition of tequila.
This is a nicely balanced wine punch that's not too sweet.
Feel free to use whatever fruits are in season.*

1 (750 ml) bottle Rioja red wine

1/2 cup freshly squeezed orange juice

1/2 cup freshly squeezed lime juice

1/4 cup simple syrup

1/2 cup Cointreau

1/2 cup tequila

Slices of apples, peaches, and limes

Place the Rioja, orange juice, lime juice, simple syrup, Cointreau, tequila, and the fruits of your choice in a large pitcher and stir to combine. Place in the fridge to chill for at least 2 hours before serving over ice.

THE LAST WORD

The Last Word was first served at the Detroit Athletic Club during Prohibition. Its slightly ethereal green color and sharp herbal edge come from the chartreuse, making it a great drink to pair with richer foods, like cheese and charcuterie.

³/₄ ounce gin
³/₄ ounce green chartreuse
³/₄ ounce freshly squeezed lime juice
³/₄ ounce maraschino liqueur

To a shaker filled three-quarters high with ice, add the gin, chartreuse, lime juice, and maraschino liqueur. Shake and strain into a chilled cocktail glass.

Serve with . . .

*A cheese board never goes out of style and is easy
to navigate without interrupting the flow of good conversation.
You don't need to spend a lot to serve a quality selection of cheeses.
Get to know the cheesemongers at your local shop or upscale grocery:
tell them what you need and what you can spend. They'll give
you tastes and advise you on what pairs well.*

A CHEESE BOARD

A good cheese board has balance: different flavors (both strong and mild) and different textures (soft, semi-soft, and hard). Have a little bit of aged cheese, like a cheddar, Manchego, or a Gouda. Add something soft, creamy, and spreadable, like a Brie or a Camembert, and something very fresh, like goat cheese, *queso fresco,* or mozzarella. Finally, add a blue cheese—a Stilton or a Gorgonzola. Three to five cheeses make for a good selection. Plan on 2 to 4 ounces of cheese per person, depending on whether or not you're serving anything else, and be sure to take the cheese out of the fridge an hour or two before serving. Cut at least a quarter of each cheese into bite-size slices or crumbles before serving so your guests won't be shy about diving in.

Choose crackers, slices of fruit-and-nut breads, or mini toasts to serve alongside. Add small bowls of olives or cornichons or serve your cheese with fruits both fresh and dried. Apple and pear slices, grapes, and figs all go well with cheese.

Definitely Daiquiris

THERE'S A GOOD REASON WHY WE OFTEN THINK of daiquiris when sipping surfside: Daiquirí is the name of a beach on the island of Cuba. In fact, it's one of the beaches where American troops landed during the Spanish-American War, not far from an iron mine of the same name. James Cox was an engineer who came to work at the mine after the war and served his guests a mixture of rum and mineral water with equal parts lemon juice and sugar, served over crushed ice. It was a drink reminiscent of the daily grog served onboard British naval ships since the 1740s. Many variations have since been introduced, including the rum, lime, and sugar combination popular throughout the Caribbean (see the Mojito, page 130).

¡salud!

THE CLASSIC DAIQUIRI

The US Navy has a long relationship with Cuba,
so it's not surprising that the daiquiri reportedly made its
stateside debut at the Army and Navy Club in Washington, D.C.,
in 1909. The drink became so popular at the club that it established
the Daiquiri Lounge, where members still sip on cocktails to this day.

2 ounces white rum

1 ounce freshly squeezed lime juice

¹/₂ ounce simple syrup

Lime wheel for garnish

To a shaker filled three-quarters full with ice, add the rum, lime juice, and syrup. Shake and strain into a chilled cocktail glass. Garnish with the lime wheel.

THE HEMINGWAY DAIQUIRI

*While the Daiquiri made a brief appearance in
F. Scott Fitzgerald's 1920 novel* This Side of Paradise,
*it was Ernest Hemingway who so favored the cocktail that
he created a version of his own. A regular at El Floridita Fish
Restaurant and Bar in Old Havana, Papa Hemingway's system
couldn't handle the sugar in the original recipe, so he substituted
grapefruit juice and maraschino liqueur. He frequently ordered
these as doubles, which became known as* Papa Dobles. *Note that
maraschino liqueur is not the juice from a jar of cherries,
but an Italian cherry-flavored liqueur.*

3 ounces white rum
1 ounce freshly squeezed lime juice
**$^1/_2$ ounce freshly squeezed
grapefruit juice**
$^1/_4$ ounce maraschino liqueur

To a shaker filled three-quarters full with ice, add the rum, lime juice, grapefruit juice, and maraschino liqueur. Shake and strain into a chilled cocktail glass.

THE FROZEN DAIQUIRI

When the frozen-Margarita machine entered the bar scene in the early 1970s, a frozen version of the classic Daiquiri soon followed and both drinks suffered from an abundance of artificial fruit flavors and sugar. Using fresh juice, fruit, and a quality rum restores this cocktail to its true status. The strawberry and banana variations opposite are very popular, but many other soft fruits, like mango, pineapple, and peaches, also work well. Avoid raspberries and blackberries, because of their seeds. Replace the Cointreau with Chambord for a raspberry flavor or, for an herbal take, substitute green chartreuse or Galliano.

1¹/₂ ounces light rum

¹/₂ ounce Cointreau

³/₄ ounce freshly squeezed lime juice

1 teaspoon simple syrup

¹/₂ cup crushed ice

Lime slice

Combine the rum, Cointreau, lime juice, and simple syrup in a blender. Add the ice and start the blender immediately. Blend until smooth and pour into a chilled cocktail or margarita glass. Garnish with the lime slice.

Variations

Frozen Strawberry Daiquiri: Add to the blender with the other ingredients ¹/₂ cup fresh strawberries if in season, or frozen if not.

Banana Daiquiri: Add one ripe sliced banana, and reduce the crushed ice to ¹/₂ cup. Puree the banana slightly with the liquid ingredients before adding the ice.

April in Paris

OOH LA LA. PARIS. *C'EST MAGNIFIQUE!* THERE'S nothing lovelier than a springtime stroll along the Seine, browsing the street sellers' stalls for some flea market fashion or perhaps a print from the next Picasso. In addition to Champagne, French cocktails are commonly based on *les apéritifs* (their version of the Italian *aperitivo*), characterized by sweeter, more floral and fruit-forward flavors. Lillet (a fortified wine), St-Germain (an elderflower liqueur), Chambord (a raspberry liqueur), and Cointreau (an orange liqueur) are some of the most famous French, or French-inspired brands to be found.

FRENCH 75

The New York Bar, located at 5, rue Daunou in Paris, has been a chic watering hole for ex-pats and the international jet set since before the First World War—and Harry MacElhone, the bar's Scottish bartender (who added his own name once he became the owner) was the source of many of the famous cocktails to emerge from this landmark location. Among them is the French 75, named for the powerful French 75mm artillery guns used during the war—it was said that the drink packed the same punch. The original recipe called for Moët Impérial Champagne, but if you choose to use another sparkling wine, we won't tell. Substituting cognac for the gin produces a richer, more complex cocktail that's perfect for a rainy day in early spring. When in France, simply ask for a Soixante Quinze.

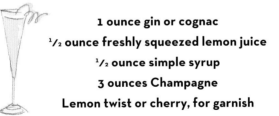

1 ounce gin or cognac
¹/₂ ounce freshly squeezed lemon juice
¹/₂ ounce simple syrup
3 ounces Champagne
Lemon twist or cherry, for garnish

To a shaker filled three-quarters full with ice, add the gin, lemon juice, and syrup. Shake well and strain into a Champagne flute. Top with the Champagne and garnish with a lemon twist.

RASPBERRY ROSE WATER FIZZ

Very loosely inspired by the Rose cocktail that was all the rage in 1920s Paris, this cocktail loses some of the sweetness of the original, but keeps the pretty, raspberry-pink hue.

2 ounces Chambord

1 ounce Cointreau

1 teaspoon rose water

1 teaspoon freshly squeezed lime juice

3 to 4 ounces sparkling water

Fill a highball glass with ice and add the Chambord, Cointreau, rose water, and lime juice. Stir with a spoon and top with sparkling water.

FRENCH BLONDE

*Dry gin is preferred here, as its botanicals won't clash
with the herbal Lillet Blanc or the floral St-Germain. Freshly
squeezed grapefruit juice provides just the right amount of sweetness.
For a red-headed hue, substitute pink grapefruit or blood orange juice.*

2 ounces freshly squeezed grapefruit juice

2 ounces Lillet Blanc

1 ounce dry gin

¹/₂ ounce St-Germain

2 dashes lemon bitters

To a shaker filled three-quarters full of ice, add the juice, Lillet, gin, St-Germain, and bitters. Shake and strain into a cocktail glass.

Serve with . . .
CRUDITÉ PLATTER WITH EASY AÏOLI

*In the south of France, this classic garlic-lemon mayonnaise is served
with just about everything, from vegetables to fish. Used as a dip for
a platter of fresh vegetables, it's the perfect accompaniment to light
cocktails such as these. The aïoli is best made the same day.*

MAKES ABOUT 1 CUP

Preheat the oven to 400°F. Remove most of the papery skin from a small head of garlic and slice off the top, exposing the cloves.

Drizzle the garlic with olive oil, wrap it in aluminum foil, and bake until very soft, about 40 minutes. When cool enough to handle, squeeze 6 of the cloves from their skins and, in a small bowl, mash them together with a pinch of coarse salt. Set aside.

Place 2 egg yolks in a food processor fitted with the steel blade. With the processor running, begin to drizzle in ½ cup extra virgin olive oil—add the oil very slowly and a little at a time (your feeder tube may have a small hole in the bottom just for this purpose). When the oil has emulsified and your mayonnaise has formed, stop the processor and add 4 teaspoons of freshly squeezed lemon juice, 1 teaspoon Dijon mustard, freshly ground white pepper to taste, and the mashed garlic. Process for a few seconds, until the garlic is well blended into the mixture. Taste and adjust the seasonings. Transfer to a small serving dish and refrigerate, covered, until ready to use.

When assembling the crudité platter, select a variety of at least 6 different colorful vegetables in season. Carrots (in rainbow colors), sliced cucumbers, and celery are always good choices, as are fresh string beans, sugar snaps, and asparagus spears (blanch them quickly, then dunk in an ice-water bath so they remain crisp). Radishes can be found in pretty varieties now—look for the long French breakfast type (leave a bit of the stem attached), or watermelon radishes that can be sliced thin. Go beyond the traditional green and red bell peppers for bright yellow, orange, and even purple; serve them sliced and seeded.

Place the dish of aïoli in the center of a serving platter and arrange the vegetables around it. Keep any extra veggies in the fridge so they'll stay crisp until it's time to replenish the selection.

An Afternoon Party

SOMEONE'S GETTING MARRIED! OR SHE'S HAVING a baby—or maybe a big birthday, or she just got a great promotion. Sooner or later, you'll have a friend who deserves to be fêted. An afternoon brunch is a great way to raise a toast on a weekend afternoon. The point is for everyone to have fun, including yourself, so set up an easy buffet and a bowl of punch and let your guests help themselves. No punch bowl? If you can't borrow one, just pour the punch into several pitchers, or investigate an inexpensive drink dispenser with a spigot.

THE GINGER BERRY

MAKES 8 TO 10 SERVINGS

Bourbon provides rich undertones in an otherwise bright and sparkling punch, which is spiced up with the addition of ginger syrup and ginger beer.

12 ounces bourbon

2 ounces Chambord

2 ounces Cointreau

4½ ounces freshly squeezed lemon juice

3 ounces ginger simple syrup (see page 22)

12 ounces ginger beer

16 ounces Prosecco

Combine the bourbon, Chambord, Cointreau, lemon juice, and simple syrup in a 1-gallon pitcher or jar. Stir well and keep cold. Just before serving, top with the ginger beer and Prosecco and stir again. Serve over ice in punch cups or rocks glasses.

WATERMELON PUNCH

This is a quintessential summer punch, best made when watermelon is in season. It's great for outdoor sipping, either on the front porch or in the backyard.

8 cups diced seedless watermelon
8 ounces tequila
8 ounces simple syrup
4 ounces freshly squeezed lime juice
16 ounces club soda
1 cup frozen strawberries
Fresh sprigs of mint, for garnish

In a blender, puree the watermelon until smooth. Pass the juice through a fine sieve over a large bowl, discarding any solids. You should have about 3 cups of juice.

Combine the juice, tequila, simple syrup, and lime juice in a 1-gallon pitcher or jar with ice. Stir well and keep cold. Just before serving, top with the club soda. Serve over ice in punch cups or rocks glasses. Drop a frozen strawberry in each glass and garnish with a sprig of mint.

Serve with . . .
A BRUNCH BUFFET SPREAD

*An easy buffet with dishes that can be purchased
or made ahead is a great way to be a guest at your own party.
Bonus: There's enough variety to please every guest.*

Choose a protein as your centerpiece: a side of poached salmon, a baked ham, or a smoked turkey breast are excellent options that can be purchased already cooked. Match bread and a sauce to your protein: mini bagels and dill sauce for the salmon, small biscuits and mustard for the ham, good rye bread and some Russian dressing for the turkey. Or make a meatless breakfast casserole, like a frittata or a strata that can be made a day ahead and served at room temperature. Add a simple tossed green salad and a fruit salad, and cupcakes or custom shower-themed cookies for dessert. As Ina Garten would say, "How easy is that?"

Mistress of Mixology

At the turn of the last century, almost half the bartenders in London were female, and none was more famous than Ada Coleman, who became head bartender of the American Bar at the Savoy Hotel in 1903. At the age of twenty-eight, she was the first (and is still the only) woman to hold that position.

Whether or not the cocktail was actually invented in the United States, by the early 1900s it was pretty clear that we'd perfected it. At the same time, England and continental Europe were playing host to Americans in record numbers, both as tourists and as romantic ex-pats. Smart hoteliers realized money could be made in serving them the cocktails they so loved at home.

The Savoy is and always has been one of the world's ritziest hotels, but it was Ada who made its bar famous, charming a clientele that included everyone from Charlie Chaplin to Mark Twain. Although the first drink she ever mixed was a Manhattan, Ada loved experimenting with mixology. Her most famous invention remains the Hanky Panky, a combination of gin, vermouth, and Fernet-Branca. Ada made the drink especially for a regular customer, Charles Hawtrey, one of the leading stage actors of the time. It's said that when he took his first sip, he downed the rest of the glass, saying, "That's the real hanky panky," which in those days meant something similar to witchcraft.

Ada left the American Bar in 1926 (rumor has it that Harry Craddock, who would go on to author the still-in-print *Savoy Cocktail Book*, didn't like sharing space behind the bar with a woman). She passed away in 1966 at the age of ninety-one.

☆ADA COLEMAN☆

When in Rome

PRENDIAMO UN APERITIVO. "LET'S GO GET AN APER-
itivo," as the Italians like to say. L'aperitivo is the social
hour between work and dinner when a cocktail (the
aperitivos in question) and light snack are meant to stim-
ulate the appetite. Aperitivo cocktails are based on the
bitter amari (see page 9) that distill spirits with secret
blends of herbs, roots, and spices. Supposedly Cleopa-
tra, via Antony and Caesar, introduced the aperitivo to
Rome and many varieties were first developed as elixers
throughout the monasteries of Europe. Today, Italian cit-
ies are filled with chic aperitivo bars where smart travelers
can eat an entire meal for the price of a cocktail.

THE AMERICANO

*The first golden age of the aperitivo hit northern Italy
in the mid-1800s, when café owners like Gaspari Campari
brought these bitter liqueurs to their bars. Campari introduced
the Milano-Torino (a mix of Campari and vermouth) in the
1860s. When American travelers began to add soda to the mix,
the drink became known as the Americano.*

1¹/₂ ounces Campari

1¹/₂ ounces sweet vermouth

2¹/₂ ounces sparkling water

Orange peel, for garnish

To a cocktail pitcher filled three-quarters full with ice, add the
Campari and vermouth and stir. Strain over ice into a rocks glass,
top with sparkling water, and garnish with an orange twist.

THE NEGRONI

The most famous of the Campari-based cocktails was first served at the Caffè Casoni in the 1920s, when Count Camillo Negroni asked that the bartender lose the sparkling water and fortify his Americano with gin. The Negroni can also be shaken and served in a cocktail glass.

1 ounce Campari

1 ounce gin

1 ounce sweet vermouth

Orange peel, for garnish

To a cocktail pitcher filled three-quarters full with ice, add the Campari, gin, and vermouth and stir. Strain over ice into a rocks glass, top with sparkling water, and garnish with an orange twist.

THE ITALIAN GREYHOUND

*Aperitivo are designed to ease digestion. This
cocktail is also quite refreshing and as elegant as its
namesake pooch. Use freshly squeezed grapefruit juice—it really
does make a difference. If you like, substitute vodka for the gin.*

5 ounces freshly squeezed grapefruit juice

1¹/₂ ounces gin

¹/₂ ounce Campari

Sprig of fresh rosemary, for garnish

To a cocktail shaker filled three-quarters full of ice, add the
grapefruit juice, gin, and Campari. Shake and pour over ice in a
highball glass. Garnish with a sprig of fresh rosemary.

Serve with . . .

THE SALUMI PLATTER

The quickest and easiest aperitivo pairing is a mix of cured meats with cheese and other accompaniments, like olives and pickled vegetables. Mix and match the selection to your taste, but here are some suggestions.

SERVES 8 TO 10

16 slices (about ³/₄ pound) each of Genoa salami, prosciutto di Parma, capicola (cured pork), and bresaola (aged, salted beef)

¹/₄ to ¹/₂ pound each of provolone or Pecorino Romano cheese, cubed

¹/₄ to ¹/₂ pound robiolo, taleggio, or bocconcini mozzarella cheeses

¹/₂ cup olives

¹/₂ cup pepperoncini or roasted red peppers

1 loaf of good Italian bread, thinly sliced

Separate the meat slices and lay them out on the outer edge of a large serving platter. Make a second ring with the cheese, then arrange the olives and vegetables in the center. Serve the bread in a separate basket.

Latin Lovers

WHETHER CELEBRATING CINCO DE MAYO OR Carnival, south of the border parties are an awesome blend of color, dancing, and great cocktails. Tequila may be the most popular choice, but rum still rules in the Caribbean. There are other bottles to explore as well, like mezcal (tequila's smoky cousin) and Pisco (the native drink of Peru and Chile). These cocktails are great for sipping on the beach or while dancing the night away.

MOJITO

At first glance, you might think there's little difference between a Daiquiri (page 106) and a Mojito, but this is a great example of how a single ingredient can change the entire flavor profile of a drink. In this case, the ingredient is mint, which is added to the classic Cuban trilogy of rum, sugar, and lime. Topped off with sparkling soda, the Mojito is one of the most refreshing cocktails to sip on a sultry summer night.

1 ounce simple syrup

8 fresh mint leaves, plus one sprig for garnish

¾ ounce freshly squeezed lime juice

2 ounces light rum

1 ounce sparkling water

Add the simple syrup and mint leaves to a shaker and muddle the two to crush the leaves. Add the lime juice (drop in the rest of the lime, if you like) and the rum and shake well. Strain into a chilled highball glass filled with ice. Top with the sparkling water and garnish with the mint sprig.

PISCO SOUR

Pisco is a colorless brandy produced in both Peru and Chile, where its manufacture is highly regulated in terms of the grapes used and the area where it's made. Because their production level is much higher, you're more likely to find Peruvian Pisco on the shelves. The Pisco Sour originated in Lima and is often called the official cocktail of Peru. The Chilean version of the drink usually does not have the garnish of bitters.

2 ounces Pisco

³/₄ ounce freshly squeezed lime juice

³/₄ ounce simple syrup

1 egg white

4 drops Angostura bitters

Place the Pisco, lime juice, syrup, and egg white in a shaker. Shake for at least 1 minute to emulsify the egg white, then add enough ice to fill the shaker two-thirds full and shake again for about 30 seconds. Strain into a cocktail glass. Add 4 drops of the bitters on top and, using a straw, swirl them decoratively across the foam.

PALOMA

Although just now becoming popular north of the border, the Paloma is the most popular cocktail in Mexico. There, it's sort of the Mexican version of rum and Coke. Tequila is poured over ice into a highball glass, sprinkled with salt, and topped with grapefruit soda (Jarritos or Squirt is the usual choice). Here's a fresher version, made with grapefruit juice and sparkling water. Use pink grapefruit juice for a Pink Paloma. For a smokier cocktail, substitute mezcal for the tequila.

Kosher salt

2 ounces tequila

2 ounces freshly squeezed grapefruit juice

¹/₂ ounce freshly squeezed lime juice

¹/₄ ounce simple syrup

2 ounces sparkling water

Lime or grapefruit slice, for garnish

Rub half the rim of a highball glass with a wedge of grapefruit and dip the rim in a plate of salt (see page 26). In a cocktail shaker filled two-thirds full with ice, combine the tequila, grapefruit juice, lime juice, and simple syrup. Shake well and strain over ice into the salt-rimmed highball glass. Top off with the sparkling water. Garnish with a slice of lime or grapefruit.

Serve with . . .
MINI TACOS

*Guacamole, salsa, and chips are a natural accompaniment
to any of these cocktails, but why not declare a taco night?*

SERVES 4 TO 6

Set out a basket of 12 store-bought mini taco shells with a
buffet of fillings: grilled sliced steak, pulled chicken or pork,
shredded red and green cabbage, sliced radishes, sliced jalapeños,
shredded cheese (cheddar or *queso fresco*), sour cream, pico de gallo,
chopped onion, sliced olives, and chopped tomatoes and avocados.

A Trip to Margaritaville

THERE ARE A LOT OF STORIES ABOUT WHO MADE the first Margarita. What's probably true is that it comes from Tijuana or someplace nearby, and it's most likely a south-of-the-border variation on the Daisy, a popular nineteenth-century drink that used brandy instead of tequila. Margarita, after all, means "daisy" in Spanish. There's no need to have margarita glasses to serve these—straight up in a cocktail glass or on the rocks in a rocks glass are both perfectly acceptable alternatives.

THE MARGARITA

The classic Margarita has been overwhelmed with many more exotic flavor combinations, but there's a refreshing simplicity to be found in the original recipe.

Lime wedge, optional
Kosher salt, optional
2 ounces tequila
³/₄ ounce Cointreau
³/₄ ounce freshly squeezed lime juice
Lime slice, for garnish

If desired, rub the rim of a cocktail or rocks glass with a wedge of lime and dip the rim in a plate of salt (see page 26). To a shaker filled three-quarters full with ice, add the tequila, Cointreau, and lime juice. Shake and strain into the prepared cocktail glass or over ice in the prepared rocks glass. Garnish with a lime slice, if desired.

Variations

Carrot Margarita: Add 4 ounces of freshly squeezed carrot juice and ½ ounce of freshly squeezed orange juice. Serve over ice in a rocks glass.

Cucumber Margarita: Replace the tequila with cucumber-infused tequila (see page 23) and garnish with a cucumber slice.

Jalapeño Margarita: Replace the simple syrup with jalapeño simple syrup (see page 22) and garnish with a thin slice of fresh jalapeño pepper.

Tamarind-Jalapeño Margarita: Make tamarind puree by blending equal amounts frozen tamarind pulp and water. Add 2 ounces of the puree and replace the simple syrup with jalapeño simple syrup (see page 22). Garnish with a thin slice of fresh jalapeño pepper.

THE FROZEN MARGARITA

Makes 4 servings

The first frozen Margarita machine—made from a soft-serve ice cream machine—was invented on May 11, 1971, by Dallas restaurateur Mariano Martinez. You can visit it at the Smithsonian's National Museum of American History in Washington, D.C. (really, that's true). Since that time, these machines have been responsible for producing a lot of artificially flavored cocktails made from super-sweet mixes. Your first taste of a homemade frozen Margarita will be a revelation. Do make more than one cocktail at a time, but make them in small batches for the proper ratio of Margarita base to ice in the blender. Making the base the day before and parking it in the freezer overnight will yield the best results—it won't freeze solid, but you'll have less dilution from the ice when you blend them before serving.

6 ounces tequila

2 ounces Cointreau

2¹/₂ ounces freshly squeezed lime juice

3 ounces simple syrup

4 cups ice

At least 8 hours or up to a week before serving, mix together the tequila, Cointreau, lime juice, and simple syrup and place in a sealed container in the freezer. When ready to serve, place the ice and tequila mixture in a blender. Blend on highest setting until completely smooth, but still slushy. Pour into cocktail glasses and serve immediately.

Variations

Frozen Strawberry Margarita: Add ¹/₂ cup of strawberry puree to the base and reduce the simple syrup by half.

Frozen Watermelon Margarita: Replace the Cointreau with St-Germain. Puree 5 cups cubed watermelon and add to the base. Reduce the simple syrup by half.

Avocado Margaritas: Puree 2 very ripe pitted and peeled avocados and add to the base. Garnish with jalapeño slices and a sprig of cilantro, if desired.

Backyard Barbecue

EVEN IF THE MENU IS SIMPLY HOT DOGS AND BURGERS on the grill, a great pitcher of cocktails is *de rigueur* for a backyard 'que. Go with the season for fruit-forward mixtures with just a touch of fresh herbs. You want a refreshing drink to balance out what's usually meat- and mayo-laden fare.

STRAWBERRY-BASIL MARGARITA

Makes 8 servings

*Fresh basil is an unexpected change from mint,
which is a worthy substitute in this recipe. Use sweet local
strawberries for the best flavor. Make the lime mixture ahead
and freeze it; make the cocktail a day ahead to let the
strawberries infuse the mix with both flavor and color.*

¹/₂ cup sugar

8 ounces freshly squeezed lime juice

8 basil leaves

16 ounces tequila

10 strawberries, hulled and cut in half

16 ounces sparkling water

In a saucepan over medium heat, combine the sugar with ½ cup water. Cook, stirring occasionally until the sugar has completely dissolved. Remove from the heat and let cool. Stir in the lime juice. Transfer the mixture to a container and place in the freezer. You can do this up to 1 week ahead of time.

To make the margarita mixture, place the basil leaves in a large glass pitcher and crush them lightly with a wooden spoon. Add the frozen lime mixture, tequila, and the strawberries. Place the pitcher in the fridge for at least 4 hours or overnight. When ready to serve, add the sparkling water and pour over ice into a punch glass or margarita glass.

LAVENDER MULE

Makes 8 servings

This is a pretty and delicate drink that would work just as well for an afternoon brunch. It has floral notes from the St-Germain and the crème de violette, with just a bit of a spicy kick from the ginger beer.

16 ounces vodka

8 ounces freshly squeezed lemon juice

8 ounces St-Germain

4 ounces crème de violette

32 ounces cold ginger beer

In a large glass pitcher, combine the vodka, lemon juice, St-Germain, and crème de violette. Chill in the fridge for at least 4 hours. When ready to serve, add the cold ginger beer and pour over ice into a punch glass or a copper mug.

SUMMER-IN-A-BOWL SALAD

Side dishes at barbecues are usually mayo-laden potato salads or slaws. This super-fresh salad takes its cue from the season itself, with fresh corn and tomatoes dressed lightly with cider vinegar. To make this vegetarian, simply omit the bacon; to give it a Tex-Mex flair, substitute cilantro for the basil, add a can of (rinsed and drained) black beans, and sprinkle a little queso cheese over the top.

Serves 4 to 6

In a large skillet, cook 4 slices of thick-cut bacon over medium heat until crisp. Remove to a paper towel–lined plate and set aside. Pour off all but 1 tablespoon of the bacon grease, turn the heat down to medium-low and add 1 medium onion, diced (about 1 cup) to the bacon drippings in the skillet. Cook, stirring occasionally, until the onion has softened, about 5 minutes. Add 2 cups freshly cut corn kernels (from about 4 ears of corn), turn the heat back up to medium, and cook, stirring occasionally, until the corn is tender and just starting to brown in spots, 7 to 10 minutes.

Remove the corn and onion mixture to a large mixing bowl and let cool for about 10 minutes. Meanwhile, cut the bacon crosswise into thin slices. Add 3 cups halved cherry tomatoes (preferably in mixed colors), the bacon, ¼ cup chopped fresh basil, and 3 tablespoons cider vinegar to the bowl with the corn. Sprinkle in a large pinch of kosher salt and freshly ground black pepper. Toss, taste, and adjust seasonings. Serve immediately at room temperature.

Tips for Better Pitcher Cocktails

- Make several batches of your cocktail mix in advance (you can do this up to 1 week ahead of time). If you're mixing the day of the party, keep them chilling in the fridge for at least 4 hours until ready to serve.

- To convert a single cocktail recipe into a pitcher's worth, take a look at the proportions and multiply from there. For example, 2 ounces liquor plus 1 ounce each of lime juice and simple syrup is a 2:1:1 ratio. For a pitcher of 8 cocktails, your mixing ratio will be 16:8:8.

- Hold off on adding any ice or carbonated beverages until just before serving (or add them separately to each glass).

- Freeze fresh fruits or even fresh juices and add them as "cubes" just before serving.

- If possible, use a glass pitcher to avoid any lingering flavors that a plastic one might hold.

Cocktails for a Rainy Day

A LITTLE RAIN SHOULDN'T DELAY THE COCKTAIL hour—just move the party indoors. Here's a selection of cocktails that are perfect to sip while it's storming outside. With a stack of grilled cheese sandwiches and a pile of DVDs, the fun can last for hours.

THE DARK AND STORMY

The Dark and Stormy is nothing like the sweet concoctions of the Caribbean. You often will see its name spelled Dark 'n Stormy, which means it contains Gosling rum. The Gosling Company of Bermuda trademarked the original recipe, so technically you can't use the 'n with another brand of rum. Use whatever rum you prefer and call it stormy-ish, but don't substitute ginger ale for the spicier ginger beer.

3 ounces ginger beer

1¹⁄₂ ounces dark rum

Lime wedge

To a rocks glass filled with ice, add the ginger beer. Top with the rum. Do not stir (the rum will float on the top and look like a storm coming in). Garnish with a squeeze of the lime.

THE CHIMNEY FIRE

This warm cocktail is perfect for a rainy night or a snowy afternoon. It's typically served in glass coffee mugs, but would also work very well in a deep cocktail glass. If you want to spice it up, try replacing ½ ounce of the Amaretto with Fireball Cinnamon Whiskey.

1¹⁄₂ ounces Amaretto

4 ounces hot apple cider

Ground cinnamon

Place the Amaretto in a coffee glass. Warm the cider and add it to the glass. Dust the top with a pinch of cinnamon.

THE NOR'EASTER

This cocktail was a specialty at the late lamented Brooklyn restaurant Char No. 4. It's a delicious cocktail any time of year, but is especially good on a late fall evening when the first frost is in the air. Be sure to use real maple syrup, not the fake corn syrup–laden bottles usually found in grocery stores.

$^1/_2$ ounce maple syrup
$^1/_2$ ounce freshly squeezed lime juice
2 ounces bourbon
2 ounces ginger beer
Lime slice, for garnish

To a shaker three-quarters full of ice, add the maple syrup, lime juice, and bourbon. Shake and strain over ice into rocks glass and top with the ginger beer. Garnish with a lime slice.

Serve with . . .
THE PERFECT
GRILLED CHEESE SANDWICH

*You've been making grilled cheese sandwiches with
Wonder Bread and Kraft Singles since you were a kid—not
that there's anything wrong with that! But here are a few tips
to take your sandwich from plain to gourmet. (A bowl of
tomato soup on the side is still definitely recommended.)*

Choose a good crusty loaf of country white or sourdough bread, but don't slice it too thick—you want a good melt, after all. If you have a cast-iron skillet, great; if not, use a heavy-bottomed frying pan. Spread a thin coat of mayonnaise on one side of both slices of bread—that's right, mayo. Any good-quality store brand will do—you'll get a crust on your sandwich like you won't believe!

Melt about a tablespoon of butter in the bottom of the pan. Place the bread, mayo-side down, in the hot pan and let it brown for about a minute. Add your cheese of choice to both pieces of bread. Once the cheese begins to melt, add any additional fillings, if desired (see list opposite) to one piece of bread and flip the other piece on top (cheese sides together). Continue to cook the sandwich until the cheese is completely melted. Transfer the sandwich to a plate and cut in half on the diagonal or into 1-inch-wide sticks.

Take Your Grilled Cheese Up a Notch

Here are some suggestions for tasty fillings that aren't too over the top (a grilled cheese should always be primarily about the cheese): mild cheddar with crispy bacon and tomato; Brie with thinly sliced pear and fig jam; provolone cheese with prosciutto; smoked Gouda with thinly sliced apple and honey; Gruyère cheese with caramelized onions. If you like a spicy sandwich, consider spreading a good, grainy mustard on the bread before laying down the cheese, or add some very thinly sliced jalapeños to the center.

Seaside Sunset

ONE OF THE BEST PARTS OF A BEACH VACATION is sitting seaside at the day's end, drink in hand, watching the sun set. It's the perfect opportunity to reflect on the activities of the day (or lack thereof) and recharge for the dinner and dancing to come, or get ready to fire up the grill for some food on a stick. These cocktails are simple, pretty, and very delicious.

TEQUILA SUNRISE

*Another cocktail whose reputation has suffered over
the years, the modern incarnation of the Tequila Sunrise hails
from 1970s Southern California. The original version, served in
the 1930s, used crème de cassis (a blackberry liqueur). Introducing
Grenadine in place of the crème de cassis made for a prettier drink, but
using Grenadine made from high-fructose corn syrup did the Sunrise
no favors. Make your own Grenadine (see page 22) and use freshly
squeezed orange juice and you'll see how tasty this drink can be.*

1¹/₂ ounces tequila
4¹/₂ ounces freshly squeezed orange juice
¹/₂ ounce Grenadine (page 22)

Pour the tequila into a highball glass filled with ice. Add
the orange juice and stir. Pour in the Grenadine (you may
want to use a spoon to guide it to the bottom of the glass).
Do not stir after adding the Grenadine. Pour into a highball glass.

AFTERNOON TEA

This is a wonderful combination of flavors that you'll find under different names in cocktail bars across the country, each with a slight variation of ingredients. The bergamot in the Earl Grey tea heightens the floral notes of the St-Germain's elderflower. If this drink becomes a new favorite, make a small bottle of Earl Grey–infused vodka to keep on hand and omit the brewed tea from the mixture.

1¹/₂ ounces vodka

1¹/₂ ounces St-Germain

1 ounce cold, brewed, Earl Grey tea

³/₄ ounce freshly squeezed lemon juice

2 ounces tonic water

To a shaker filled three-quarters up with ice, add the vodka, St-Germain, tea, and lemon juice. Shake well and strain over ice into a rocks glass. Top with the tonic water.

Serve with . . .

*Kebabs are an easy summer snack to serve with drinks
before dinner, or you can add a salad and call it a meal. Mix
and match your proteins and vegetables based on what looks best
at the farmers' market. If you're using bamboo skewers, give them a
30-minute soak in water beforehand, so they don't burn on the grill.*

SWEET AND SPICY
CHICKEN KEBABS

Serves 8 to 10

Heat an outdoor grill or a grill pan to medium heat. Cut, core, and peel a fresh pineapple and cut the fruit into 1-inch chunks. Clean a large red onion and cut into thick slices and then 1-inch chunks. In a mixing bowl, combine ¼ cup each of olive oil and maple syrup, 1 tablespoon harissa paste, 2 teaspoons cumin seeds, and salt and freshly ground black pepper. Cut 4 boneless, skinless chicken breasts into 1-inch cubes. Add the chicken cubes to the spice mixture and toss to coat. Lightly drizzle the pineapple and onion with olive oil and thread them on the skewers, alternating with the chicken pieces. Grill, turning frequently, until the chicken juices run clear, about 8 minutes.

GRILLED FRUIT KEBABS

Serves 8 to 10

Heat an outdoor grill or a grill pan to medium heat. Choose 4 or 5 of the following: about 2 cups each of fresh strawberries, pineapple, peaches, nectarines, watermelon, cantaloupe, or honeydew, cut into 1-inch chunks. Thread the fruit, alternating the varieties, onto skewers. Squeeze fresh lime juice over all and sprinkle lightly with salt and freshly ground black pepper. Place on the grill and cook, turning every 30 seconds, until the fruit softens slightly and takes on grill marks, 2 to 4 minutes.

From Russia, with Love

A TRIUMPH OF SALESMANSHIP, THE MOSCOW MULE is the direct result of a desire to get Americans to drink more vodka. Invented in the 1940s to push liquor sales, even the now ubiquitous copper mug was part of the pitch—the mugs could be branded with the vodka brand (Smirnoff). Whether it's the copper mug or the drink's adaptability (see Lavender Mule, page 143, and the variations on pages 160-161), the Mule has seen a great surge in popularity in the past few years. The copper mug will keep the drink icy cold, but a Mule is perfectly comfortable in a rocks glass as well.

THE MOSCOW MULE

For reasons lost to cocktail history, drinks that mix a base spirit with ginger beer and a citrus juice are often called mules or bucks, perhaps because of the "kick" provided by the spicy ginger beer. A Moscow Mule was often also served under the moniker Vodka Buck.

2 ounces vodka

¹/₂ ounce freshly squeezed lime juice

4 to 6 ounces ginger beer

Lime wedge, for garnish

To a cocktail shaker filled three-quarters full of ice, combine the vodka and lime juice. Shake and strain into a copper mug or rocks glass filled with crushed ice. Top with the ginger beer and garnish with lime.

Variations

London Mule: Muddle 2 to 3 mint leaves in the shaker before adding the ice, and replace the vodka with an equal amount of dry gin. Strain into a highball glass filled with ice and garnish with a wedge of lime.

Mexican Mule: Replace the vodka with an equal amount of tequila and add ¹/₂ ounce jalapeño simple syrup (page 22). Strain into a highball glass filled with ice and garnish with a thin slice of jalapeño pepper and a wedge of lime.

Fruit-Flavored Mule: Add 2 ounces of pureed fruit (such as watermelon, mango, peach, or strawberry) or fruit juice to the classic recipe. If you're using a tart fruit, consider adding 1 ounce of a complementary-flavored simple syrup, like vanilla, basil, or cinnamon.

KENTUCKY MULE

This is a great drink for Derby Day. For an even more Southern take, add 1 ounce of peach nectar to the shaker with the bourbon and lime juice.

2 to 3 mint leaves, plus 1 sprig for garnish
2 ounces bourbon
¹/₂ ounce freshly squeezed lime juice
4 to 6 ounces ginger beer

In a cocktail shaker, muddle the mint leaves. Fill the shaker three-quarters full with ice, and add the bourbon and lime juice. Shake and strain into a copper mug or rocks glass filled with crushed ice. Top with the ginger beer and garnish with a sprig of mint.

Bubble, Bubble, Toil, and Trouble

ONCE YOU'VE OUTGROWN TRICK-OR-TREATING, Halloween cocktails are the next best things for getting in the spooky spirit. Pinterest pages are filled with elaborate concoctions garnished with vampire fangs and plastic eyeballs, but these tricks are still best for kids. This pair of cocktails can be the scary centerpiece of a sophisticated gathering. Decorate with carved pumpkins and turn the seeds into a spicy accompaniment (see page 166).

CORPSE REVIVER NO. 2

Corpse Reviver cocktails were a popular hangover cure in the late 1800s, but most of the formulas didn't survive Prohibition. Version number 2 is a slightly sweet and citrusy drink that gets a dash of herbs from the absinthe. For Halloween, blood orange juice would make a great substitute for the lemon juice and, while not traditional, a cherry makes a pretty garnish in place of the orange peel.

1 ounce gin

1 ounce Cointreau

1 ounce Lillet Blanc

1 ounce freshly squeezed lemon juice

$\frac{1}{8}$ teaspoon absinthe

Orange peel, for garnish

Fill a shaker three-quarters full with ice. Add the gin, Cointreau, Lillet, lemon juice, and absinthe. Shake well and strain into a chilled cocktail glass. Garnish with the orange peel.

VAMPIRE'S KISS

*There are a few different cocktails that carry this name,
most of them as sweet as any treat from the candy bowl.
This one is a slightly fruitier version of a Cosmo, and you can add
extra sex appeal by rimming the glass with red sugar.*

1 lime wedge
Red sugar for rimming the glass (see 26)
2 ounces vodka
1¹/₂ ounces Chambord
4 ounces cranberry juice
¹/₂ ounce freshly squeezed lime juice
4 pomegranate seeds, for garnish

Rim a chilled cocktail glass with the lime wedge and red sugar. Fill
a shaker three-quarters full with ice. Add the vodka, Chambord,
cranberry, and lime juice. Shake well and strain into the prepared
cocktail glass. Drop the pomegranate seeds into the bottom of the glass.

Serve with . . .
SPICY PUMPKIN SEEDS

Halloween drinks tend to be a little sweet, so it's nice to have
an accompaniment that brings some heat. These spicy pumpkin seeds
are a great way to use what's come out of your pumpkins.

SERVES 4

Preheat the oven to 300°F. In a colander, rinse the seeds scraped from 1 large pumpkin to remove any pumpkin flesh or strings (the average pumpkin yields about 1 cup of seeds). Spread in a single layer across a greased rimmed baking sheet. Roast for 30 minutes. In a small bowl, mix together 1½ tablespoons ancho chili powder, 1 tablespoon kosher salt, 1 teaspoon dried oregano, and 1 teaspoon smoked paprika.

Place the toasted seeds in a large bowl. Toss with 2 tablespoons canola oil and then the chili powder mixture. Spread evenly on a rimmed baking sheet and bake for 8 to 10 minutes, stirring once. Let cool and store in an airtight container.

Jazz Babies

THE ROARING TWENTIES RANG IN THE JAZZ AGE and the music didn't end until the stock market fell in 1929. Prohibition couldn't stop this generation's taste for cocktails, which became even more popular in the elicit speakeasies of the day. Many of the drinks from this time entered the classics category, while others are being rediscovered by the craft bartenders of today.

PINK SHIMMY

*This is a version of the Pink Lady cocktail, replacing
the single egg white with a touch of cream. A popular cocktail
of the 1920s and '30s with both men and women, it wasn't until
much later that pink drinks were spurned as being too feminine.
Sure, it looks pretty, but this is one serious cocktail.*

1¹/₂ ounces dry gin

1 ounce Laird's AppleJack

³/₄ ounce freshly squeezed lemon juice

³/₄ ounce cream

¹/₄ ounce Grenadine (see page 22)

Cherry for garnish

Add the gin, AppleJack, lemon juice, cream, and Grenadine
to a shaker and shake well to emulsify the cream. Add enough ice to
fill the shaker by three-quarters and shake again. Place a cherry
in the bottom of a chilled cocktail glass. Strain the cocktail into
the glass.

SIDECAR

Another classic cocktail from behind Harry's New York Bar in Paris, this drink takes its name from the motorcycle sidecars that were so prevalent in World War I. The 1:1:1 ratio of cognac, Cointreau, and lemon is traditional, but some prefer to double the cognac quotient. If you like a sweeter drink, consider rimming half the glass with sugar (see page 26).

1 ounce cognac

1 ounce Cointreau

1 ounce freshly squeezed lemon juice

Lemon peel, for garnish

To a shaker filled three-quarters full with ice, add the cognac, Cointreau, and lemon juice. Shake and strain into a chilled cocktail glass. Garnish with a twist of lemon, if desired.

AVIATION

This early 1920s cocktail is as lavender blue as the skies that were dotted by those fearless early pilots in their flying machines. Harry Craddock omitted the crème de violette from the recipe printed in his influential Savoy Cocktail Book, *and the overly sour result never really caught on. Without the Aviation to support it, crème de violette also fell out of favor and for many years was not available in the United States. It's made a comeback in the last decade and, like the equally floral St-Germain, is increasingly finding its way into craft cocktails.*

2 ounces gin
³/₄ ounce freshly squeezed lemon juice
¹/₂ ounce maraschino liqueur
¹/₄ ounce crème de violette
Brandied cherry (see page 56), for garnish

To a shaker filled three-quarters high with ice, add the gin, lemon juice, maraschino liqueur, and crème de violette. Shake well and strain into a chilled cocktail glass. Garnish with a brandied cherry.

Serve with . . .
BACON AND BLEU CHEESEBALL

The cocktail hour brought with it the canapé, and every good home hostess had an arsenal of recipes for little salty tidbits that could be thrown together from pantry staples. Cream cheese was stuffed into ribs of celery, cold ham was served atop toast points, and anything could be placed upon a cracker. When serving drinks of the period, why not pair them with some fun retro hors d'oeuvres? Here is a classic cheese ball, updated with modern flavors. If you don't care for bleu cheese, substitute an equal amount of goat cheese.

SERVES 8 TO 10

Toast ½ cup chopped pecans in a dry frying pan for several minutes, until fragrant. Set aside to cool. Fry 4 slices thin-cut, applewood-smoked bacon until crisp. Remove to paper towel–lined plate to cool, then finely chop and set aside.

Place 2 (8-ounce) packages of room-temperature cream cheese, 4 ounces crumbled bleu cheese, 4 ounces shredded sharp cheddar cheese, 2 tablespoons dry white wine, and ¼ cup minced shallots in a food processor and mix until fully blended. Add the bacon and pulse several times.

Shape the cheese mixture into a ball and roll it in the toasted pecans. Wrap in plastic wrap and refrigerate at least 4 hours or overnight. Serve with wafer-type crackers, preferably Ritz.

What to Wear to a Cocktail Party

As with just about every aspect of cocktail lore, there's great debate as to who threw the first cocktail party. Some say it took place in London, but much more delightful is the story of Mrs. Julius S. Walsh Jr. of St. Louis, Missouri, who, in May 1917, invited fifty guests to her home on a Sunday afternoon for one hour of cocktails and tidbits. The local paper declared it "an instant hit."

Surely not long after, women began to wonder what one would wear to such an event. Leave it to Coco Chanel to come up with the answer. In 1926, *Vogue* magazine published a picture of a short, simple black dress designed by Chanel, calling it her "Ford," an allusion to Ford's Model T automobile. Like the car, this little black dress was accessible, and would look good on every woman. Although Christian Dior would be the first to use the term "cocktail dress" in the late 1940s, it was Chanel who provided women with a classic sheath that's perfect for any occasion, but especially for the cocktail hour.

Chanel "Ford"

Dior

Princess

Body-Con

A-line

Shift

Strapless

Sheath

Empire

Home for the Holidays

FROM THE ANNUAL COMPANY BLOWOUT TO TRAD-itional family dinners, the holiday season is filled with festive occasions. It's also a great opportunity to invite friends and neighbors in for a simple evening of cheer and good wishes. Whether serving memorable eggnog that can be made months in advance or a pretty Champagne cocktail in a seasonable shade of red, simply add a holiday cookie plate and you're all set. Did someone say "cookie swap"?

GEORGE WASHINGTON'S EGGNOG

Makes 8 to 12 servings

In addition to being the father of our country, George Washington was also a respected distiller of his day, well known for his own eggnog recipe. The longer it's aged, the better it tastes. If stored properly—in tightly sealed containers at or below 40°F (i.e., the bottom shelf of your fridge)—the nog can be safely aged for up to a year. It's a good idea to sterilize the container before adding the nog, and give it a shake every few days to keep everything well mixed. This eggnog is rich and tasty and deceptively potent, so take care to enjoy it responsibly.

16 ounces (2 cups) brandy

8 ounces (1 cup) rye whiskey

8 ounces (1 cup) rum

4 ounces (¹/₂ cup) sherry

1 dozen eggs

³/₄ cup sugar

1 quart whole milk

1 quart heavy cream

In a large pitcher, mix together the brandy, rye whiskey, rum, and sherry. Separate the eggs, placing the yolks in one large bowl and the whites in another. Beat the yolks, then add the sugar and mix well. Add the mixed liquors, a little at a time, while stirring slowly. Add the milk and cream, slowly beating to combine. In a separate bowl, beat the egg whites until stiff and fold slowly into the mixture.

Pour into a 1-gallon glass container with a tight-fitting lid and set in the refrigerator for at least three weeks or up to a year.

POINSETTIA

As Christmassy as the flower that it's named for, the Poinsettia is a perfect Champagne cocktail for the holidays: bright and bubbly, and a light accompaniment to all the season's eatings.

¹/₂ ounce Cointreau

3 ounces cranberry juice

Champagne or sparkling wine (see page 181)

Fresh raspberries, cranberries, or pomegranate seeds, for garnish

Pour the Cointreau and cranberry juice into a chilled Champagne flute and stir well. Top with Champagne. Drop a raspberry or two into the glass for garnish.

Serve with...
CHRISTMAS COOKIES

*If you're in the habit of baking cookies for the holidays,
then you're good to go. Otherwise, visit the local bakery for
a tray of holiday favorites. Biscotti in a variety of flavors are
also a good choice—they're perfect for dunking in eggnog.*

Types of Sparkling Wine

Champagne is only Champagne when it comes from the Champagne region of France. By law, it can only be made—via the Champagne method, in which the second fermentation takes place in the bottle—from Chardonnay, Pinot Noir, and Pinot Meunier grapes. A good rule of thumb is to choose a better quality alternative sparkling wine over a cheap Champagne.

Cava is a sparkling wine, primarily from the Catalonia region of Spain. Available in white and rosé, cava is made by the Champagne method, but can't legally be called "Champagne." Freixenet is one of the most recognizable labels.

Prosecco is a white sparkling wine produced in and around the Veneto region of northeast Italy. Traditionally made from Glera grapes indigenous to the region, it can be found in *spumante* (sparkling) and *frizzante* (semi-sparkling) versions. Prosecco's second fermentation takes place in stainless-steel tanks, making it less expensive to produce than Champagne. Prosecco has become increasingly popular and very good bottles can be found at reasonable prices.

Champagne and other sparkling wines are described by their level of sweetness, from brut nature (very dry, with no added sugar), through extra brut, brut, extra dry, sec (dry), demi-sec, and sweet (*doux* or *dulce*).

It's My Party

HAVING READ THIS FAR, HOPEFULLY YOU ARE NOW
inspired to channel your inner bartender and create your own specialty
cocktails. Perhaps you want a signature cocktail—a drink that friends can
always count on being offered in your home. Or you're hosting a special
event and want a cocktail that will honor the occasion. Or maybe you just
want to have a little fun with friends. Set up a mini mixology lab and host
an "invent your own cocktail" evening. Here are a few suggestions to make
the process user-friendly.

DON'T WORRY ABOUT STARTING FROM SCRATCH.

One of the easiest ways to create a new cocktail is to base it on another
drink. Swap out one ingredient for another, choose a different liquor
or liqueur, add a complementary flavor. It may be as simple as using an
infused liquor in place of the original and changing up the garnish.

YOU CAN ALSO CREATE A NEW VARIATION ON A CLASSIC.

There are so many variations on the Bloody Mary (page 90), Martini (page
66), Daiquiri (page 106), Margarita (page 136), Moscow Mule (page 160),
and other classic cocktails that you can look to for inspiration. Do stay
true to a classic liquor profile, though. There is no such thing as a Bourbon
Martini or a Vodka Manhattan.

Have a vision.

To get started, create a mental vision board of what your cocktail should be. If you're designing a drink for a specific event, there are plenty of cues.

Be Colorful: Holiday drinks can be based on color (orange for Thanksgiving, blue for Hanukkah, red for Christmas, even green for St. Patrick's Day). If you're hosting a bridal shower, match the color theme of the wedding. For a baby shower, you might want pink and blue cocktails. Oscar parties lend themselves to golden cocktails. Always achieve colors naturally, and only use food dye when tinting sugar to rim a glass (see page 26).

Think seasonally: Design your cocktail in harmony with the time of year (there's no rule that you can't have a signature drink for all four seasons). Autumn cocktails call for maple syrup, apples, and spices like cinnamon and nutmeg. Consider a drink that can be served warm. Cranberry is synonymous with fall and winter both. Spring and summer cocktails are more fruit- and vegetable-forward. Strawberries, watermelon, cucumber, and herbal combinations are refreshing choices. It's somewhat true that brown liquors (rye, bourbon, scotch) are better for the winter, while white or gold liquors (gin, vodka, tequila, rum) are best for the summer months, but that's partly a matter of taste.

Think about your favorite flavor profiles: Cocktails can be spicy, smoky, herbal, bitter, sweet, or a combination of more than one. These flavors can be achieved in a number of ways. Take smoky, for example. Mezcal is distilled from the agave plant, like tequila, but it has a smoky flavor. Lapsang souchong tea offers a less-expensive alternative. Its leaves are dried over smoky pine fires, giving the tea a very distinctive, smoky flavor. Use it to infuse liquor, simple syrup, or even brew the tea and freeze it as ice cubes for your smoky cocktail.

Liqueurs and amari are usually pricey, so think carefully before making one part of your signature drink. If you have a flavor profile in mind, try to achieve it through infusions, syrups, or bitters first.

Choose a favorite subject and bring those traits to your cocktail: You can design a drink around a favorite character, novel, or author. Likewise, a favorite movie or television show, actor or actress, or character can be the inspiration (see the Stars Hollow, page 38; Mother of Dragons, page 39; Crazy Eyes, page 40; and Frankly Bitter, page 41). The Bellini (page 31) is said to have been inspired by the color of a robe in one of the artist's paintings. Your next museum trip or walk in the park may spark fresh ideas.

Make your cocktail about you: If you have red hair, perhaps your cocktail recipe will be driven by that color, or flavored with ginger. Or design a drink around your ethnic heritage with liqueurs from your ancestral homeland (see the Irish Italian, page 61, or Pisco Sour, page 131). Build a cocktail around a talent or hobby that you're known for.

Keep it simple.

With a few exceptions, the cocktails in this book have three to four ingredients and that's more than enough. Have your base alcohol balanced by equal parts sweet and sour—simple syrup and lime juice, for example. Use the standard ratio of 2:1:1—that's 2 ounces of the base liquor to 1 ounce sweet and 1 ounce sour. You can stop there or add more depth with a complementary flavor enhancer like a liqueur or bitters. A garnish should be there for a reason: to further enhance the taste of the drink.

Shaken or stirred?

Drinks made with juice or other noncarbonated mixers should be shaken with ice. Drinks that are made with egg whites or cream must be shaken for at least 2½ minutes so that they emulsify properly. Drinks that are 100-percent alcohol are stirred with ice in a cocktail pitcher.

Choose appropriate ingredients.

As stated at the beginning of the book, you don't have to reach for the top shelf, especially when making a mixed drink. Many of the very best liquors are more suited to sipping neat or on the rocks. Start your experimentation with mid-price liquors and when you find a recipe you like, upgrade from there.

Don't succumb to using a mix, or bottled ingredients.

Always use freshly squeezed juices, even if you buy them at the local juice bar. Simple syrups are very easy to make, and you'll avoid drinking high-fructose cocktails.

What's in a Name?

Your custom cocktail needs a name—a process that is an art in itself and a lot of fun. The name could very simply describe what's in your drink, like a Gin and Tonic (page 82), but in a more artistic way. A cocktail composed of Earl Grey-infused vodka could be a Bergamot Tea-ni (picking up on the botanical that gives the tea its distinctive flavor), or a Grey Earl, or a Mad Hatter (from Alice's famous tea party).

Keep your vision board in mind and follow the same creative process. Maybe your cocktail is a Christmas Tree, a Red Devil, a Baby's Rattle, or named in honor of the bride-to-be. Just as the name can describe the ingredients, it can also reflect the flavor profile. Think about being a Smoky Redhead, a Spicy Ginger, or a Sweet Kitty. Name the cocktail after yourself, your pet, or even where you live—how about the Lombard Twist, the Broadway Baby, or the Nightmare on Elm Street?

Just remember, a great cocktail is a great cocktail, no matter what it's called.

Acknowledgments

TO EVERYONE AT RUNNING PRESS, ESPECIALLY MY LOVELY editor, Cindy De La Hoz, and talented designer; Amanda Richmond.

To Marisa Bulzone, for your brilliant writing. You were such a joy and pleasure to work with.

To my agent, Fran Black, for your creativity and endless support.

To Jason, for your love, humor, and knowing when to make me a perfectly ice-cold martini with three blue cheese-stuffed olives.

To my incredible family, for being as excited about this book as I am.

To my friends, for your encouragement and unconditional love.

And finally, to my dad, for your contagious energy and never-ending inspiration. "Up your pant leg!" (Cheers!). xo

Index

189

191